The **Interviewing** Guidebook

The **Interviewing** Guidebook

Second Edition

Joseph A. DeVito

Hunter College of the
City of New York

Allyn & Bacon
Boston   New York   San Francisco
Mexico City   Montreal   Toronto   London   Madrid   Munich   Paris
Hong Kong   Singapore   Tokyo   Cape Town   Sydney

Allyn & Bacon
is an imprint of

www.pearsonhighered.com

ISBN-10: 0-205-73051-5

ISBN-13: 978-0-205-73051-3

Brief Contents

Contents

Specialized Contents

Worksheets

Interviewing Exercises

Welcome to
The **Interviewing**
Guidebook

Interviewing is one of the most important communication skills you can learn. It's crucial to getting the job you want, and ultimately the career you're preparing for right now. But interviewing skills will also help you obtain information and achieve a wide variety of communication goals identified throughout this discussion.

The Interviewing Guidebook focuses on two major types of interviews: the information-gathering interview, and the employment interview (along with the job résumé and the letters that are an essential part of the interview process). Other types of interviews are mentioned in passing (and guides to further exploration of these types are given) but they are not discussed in detail here.

The discussions of the informative and job interviews emphasize the skills you'll need to be successful in your own interviewing. Along with the text, which identifies the major interviewing skills and provides lots of examples to illustrate what works and what doesn't, are a variety of features to further help you master the skills of interviewing:

- **Interview Worksheets** provide guides for preparing both the information-gathering and the employment interviews. These will help you clarify your thoughts about the interview and identify the major questions you need to consider for each type of interview.

- **Interviewing Exercises** are included to help you work actively with the concepts discussed here.

- **Online Help** notes identify useful websites.

- **Interviewing Choice Point** scenarios will help you apply your interviewing skills to different situations.

- **Quotations** sprinkled throughout are designed to serve as "pause points," places in your reading where you'll find it useful to stop reading and ponder the implications of the quotation for your own interviewing experiences.

New to This Edition

A variety of improvements have been made in this second edition. Among the most significant are these:

- A restructured section on Types of Interviews now includes discussions of phone, online, and group interviews—all of which are becoming more popular in business hiring practices.

- The discussion of interpersonal communication skills has been expanded and moved to an earlier position in the text.

- A discussion of the informational research interview, which allows you to collect information to help you in the employment interview, has been added, providing a useful transition between the information and employment interviews.

- Worksheets for The Cheat Sheet (to help you in any type of interview but especially the phone interview) and Communication Skill Set (to help you identify those communication skills that you may wish to mention during your interview) are now included.

- Exercises on Classifying Types of Questions and the Best and the Worst (to help you rehearse commonly asked questions) have been added. The Interview for Analysis remains but has been recast as an exercise for analyzing interviewing confidence.

- New Online Helps, Interviewing Choice Points, and quotations have also been added throughout the text.

Joseph A. DeVito
jadevito@earthlink.net
http://tcbdevito.blogspot.com
www.pearsonhighered.com/devito

The **Interviewing** Guidebook

You'll no doubt find yourself in a wide variety of interview situations throughout your social and professional life. And, as you'll see throughout this brief book, your effectiveness in this form of communication will prove crucial in helping you achieve many of your life goals. This discussion covers three main topics:

1. the nature of interviewing, its characteristics, the nature of questions and answers, and the general types of interviews;

2. the information-gathering interview and the strategies to follow for greatest effectiveness; and

INTERVIEWING CHOICE POINT Throughout the text, Interviewing Choice Points are presented in the margins. The aim of these notes is to stimulate you to pause and reflect on what your options are and on what you'd say in each of these specific interview situations.

3. the employment interview and how you can best present yourself in this interview and in your résumé and cover letter.

Unless I miss my guess, you're going to find interviewing an exciting and eminently practical communication skill. Good luck.

Unit 1
The Nature of Interviewing

The **interview** is a particular form of communication in which you interact largely through a question-and-answer format to achieve a specific goal or function. Here are just a few such instances:

- A salesperson tries to persuade a client to buy a new car.
- A teacher talks with a student about the reasons the student failed the course.
- A grandchild talks with grandparents in an effort to record family history.
- A counselor talks with a family about their communication problems.
- A recent graduate applies to Cisco for a job in the product development division.
- A doctor interviews a patient about past illnesses.
- A journalist interviews a political candidate.
- A Senate committee interviews the FCC chair.
- A building owner talks with a potential apartment renter.
- A minister talks with a church member about a membership drive.
- A lawyer examines a witness during a trial.
- A department's personnel committee interviews an application for a teaching position.
- A theatrical agent talks with a producer.

- A client discusses the qualities desired in a potential mate with a dating service employee.

- An employer talks with an employee about the reasons for terminating employment.

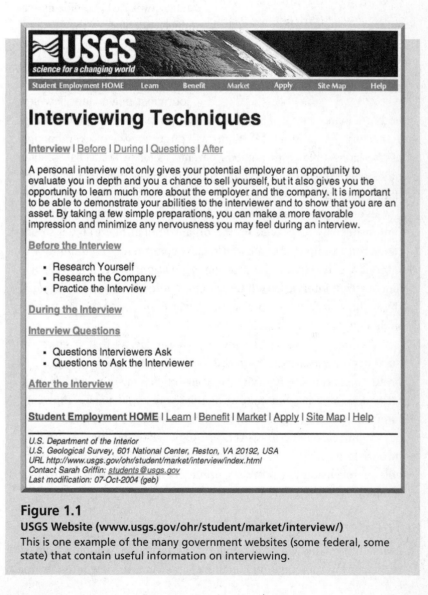

Figure 1.1
USGS Website (www.usgs.gov/ohr/student/market/interview/)
This is one example of the many government websites (some federal, some state) that contain useful information on interviewing.

As you can see, interviews serve a wide variety of functions—to persuade you to buy or sell, to inform you or to gain information from you, to counsel and support, and to uncover the truth, for example.

> *In the hands of a skilled practitioner [the interview] is like a sharp knife that can cut away all the fat of irrelevant detail to get to the meat of the subject.*
>
> —JACK GRATUS

Most interviews follow a two-person structure, but team interviews are becoming increasingly popular. In the media—on "Nightline," for example—several journalists might interview a political candidate or one journalist might interview several candidates. On the ubiquitous television talk show, Oprah Winfrey, Jerry Springer, or Montel Williams will often interview several people at the same time. And anxious parents (and, in some cases, even members of the extended family) might interview their teenager's first dating partner.

In employment situations, team interviews are extremely important, especially as you go up the organizational hierarchy. It's common, for example, for an academic department or committee to interview a candidate for a teaching position, often followed by a similar team interview with the administration. In business organizations, three or four vice presidents might interview a candidate for a middle-management position.

The main advantage of the team interview is that it gives the audience or the organization different viewpoints and perspectives on the person being interviewed. It also helps ensure that the interview does not lag but follows a relatively rapid pace—especially important when the interview is on the Internet or on television.

Team interviews, however, are expensive and may degenerate into what may appear to be interrogations, a quality that may be desirable on television but is inappropriate in an employment setting (see Kanter, 1995).

The Interview Process

In much the same way that you look at perception, listening, conversation, or interpersonal relationships, you can also view interviewing

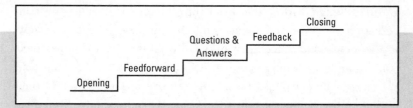

Figure 1.2

The Stages of the Interview

This model is designed to highlight the *general* process of interviewing; but it needs to be modified on the basis of the specific interview in which you find yourself. View the stages as general categories that illustrate the natural progression of most interviews.

As you review these stages realize that even though you are meeting the interviewer for the first time, the interviewer may already have considerable information about you—from your résumé, your letters and e-mails, and much of your social networking posts. Also, the interview is not really completed at the closing; rather there is follow-up that must be done (for example, a thank-you letter), a topic covered later in this book.

as a series of stages: opening, feedforward, question-and-answer format, feedback, and closing (see Figure 1.2).

During all interviews, be especially alert for transitional cues that signal a move from one stage of the interview to the next. Don't continue to dwell on preliminaries after the interviewer has signaled a readiness to move to the next stage, for instance. As an interviewer, give cues that are easily understandable, and as an interviewee, watch carefully for and respond appropriately to these cues.

Opening At the first stage, interviewee and interviewer meet; the interview opens at that moment. Although this is an introductory stage and may seem to involve a "mere" exchange of common courtesies such as *hellos* and an exchange of names, an invitation to sit down, and perhaps a comment or two on the weather, this is a crucial part of the interview and you'll want to be at your best here as well as during the main phase of the interview. The conversation taking place at this stage is clearly preliminary and is more designed to make the situation comfortable than to communicate job-related information.

Feedforward   After this brief introductory exchange, the conversation narrows and focuses on the purpose of the interview. It provides a kind of feedforward as to what is going to happen next (for example, "I want to go over a few things on your résumé and then ask you a few questions about your training and so on"). You'll notice on the late-night talk shows that there is usually some preliminary communication and then the host focuses the interview on the real purpose the celebrity is there: "So I see you have a new movie out."

Question-and-Answer Session   Once the interview is focused, the question-and-answer session, the essential part of the interview, begins. If this is an information-gathering interview, then the questions will seek information and the interviewee will provide it, it is hoped. If this is an employment interview, the interviewer will attempt to discover your strengths and your weaknesses to get an impression of how suitable you'd be for the position, while you will attempt to present yourself as most suitable. At the same time, you may want to ask questions about the position, benefits, and so on. Most of the suggestions made throughout this book are addressed to this stage.

Feedback   After the questions are asked and the answers given, the interviewer will provide some basic feedback. Usually the feedback comes in the form of some positive comments and perhaps a summary of some significant part of the interview: "It was a pleasure meeting you. You sure seem like a person who thinks thoroughly before making decisions."

Closing   The closing is generally mixed in with the feedback and might go something like this: "Thanks for coming in to see us. I'm going to review your file and then I have a few more people to interview. So we'll be in touch with you within the next few weeks."

In all interviews, be especially alert to **leave-taking cues.** It's important that you recognize when the interviewer is saying the interview is over. Generally, it's best not to try to prolong the interview after clear leave-taking cues are given.

Types of Interviews

Interviews vary in structure, use varied channels, and may be individual or group. Each of these qualities of interviews is detailed below.

Interview Structures   Interviews vary from relatively informal talks that resemble everyday conversations to those in which rigidly prescribed questions are asked in a set order (Hambrick, 1991). Depending on your specific purpose, you can select the interview structure, or combine various types to create a unique interview structure, that best fits your needs.

The Informal Interview.   In the **informal interview,** two friends might discuss what happened on their respective dates or employment interviews: *So tell me what happened? . . . And then what? . . . So what did you say? . . .* This type of interview resembles conversation; a general theme for the interview is chosen in advance but the specific questions are formed during the interaction. You use this type of interview to obtain information informally, as when you question another student regarding what happened in a class you missed. These interviews are highly nondirective—one person does not direct the other; rather, each person responds much as she or he wants.

The Guided Interview.   In the **guided interview,** a guest on "The Tonight Show" might be interviewed about a new CD or a person might be interviewed for a job: *I see you have a new movie out. It looks like it's going to be a big hit. You play a senator. . . . Yeah, I play a senator from Hawaii who comes to Washington for the first time. And then the fun starts. . . .* Here the topics are chosen in advance but specific questions and wording are guided by the ongoing interaction. The guided interview is useful because it ensures maximum flexibility in and responsiveness to the dynamics of the situation, though it is somewhat more directive than the informal interview.

The Standard Open Interview.   The **standard open interview** might be used for interviewing several candidates for a job; you may want to ask each of them the exact same question so you can compare their responses: *We're taking on a new client, a paint company that wants to compete with the major manufacturers, so we'll need a total advertising plan in three months. Any ideas?* Open-ended questions and their order are selected in advance. This type of interview would be useful when standardization is needed, when you want to be sure to ask each person the same question in exactly the same way. This interview is highly directive; the interviewer guides the interview closely.

The Quantitative Interview. In the **quantitative interview**, a researcher might survey students' political opinions. In this form, questions and their order are selected in advance, as are the possible response categories—for example, A, B, C, D; agree–disagree; check from 1 to 10: *How often do you go to the dentist? (a) less than once a year, (b) once a year, (c) once every six months, (d) more often than every six months.* The quantitative interview is useful when statistical analyses are to be performed and when large amounts of information are to be collected. This is the most directive of all interviews; there is usually little opportunity to comment outside the rigidly prescribed format. Many of the popular books on relationships, sexual behavior, and child rearing, for example, are based on surveys that enable researchers to draw conclusions as to the age at which boys and girls start dating, the frequency of sexual behavior, and the most common child-rearing practices.

Interview Channels   Interviews may take place face-to-face, by phone, and online (generally through e-mail). Each of these channels requires special handling.

Face-to-Face. The face-to-face channel is perhaps the one that comes to mind most readily when you think of interviewing and most of the recommendations in this book are directed at this type of interview.

Phone. Often, an organization will interview a number of candidates by phone and then, on the basis of these phone calls, decide which candidates to invite for face-to-face interviews. Here are a few suggestions for making this phone interview more effective and increasing your chances of being invited to a face-to-face interview.

1. Make sure your connection is clear. This is not the time to use a cell phone that fades in and out. Set up a quiet space without any distractions. Avoid having this conversation at your workplace; you may not be able to control the interruptions or to speak as privately as you might like.
2. Have in front of you water to clear your throat if necessary, a pen and paper to write down important information, and a "cheat sheet" (see the accompanying box).

THE CHEAT SHEET

(for an employment interview)

The "cheat sheet" is a useful aid to the phone interview, or to any other interview. You create the cheat sheet and review it before going into an interview or keep it in front of you during a phone interview. The interviewer never sees this sheet. The **cheat sheet** contains the information you want to be sure to cover in the interview. Keep it short and simple; if it's too long it may be difficult to review before the interview or use during the phone call and may, in fact, get in the way of sounding spontaneous. Although each job and each candidate will require a somewhat different cheat sheet, it will generally look something like this:

Thank the Interviewer!

Experiences to mention
Record here any experiences you've had that might be relevant to the position—for example, relevant travel, leadership positions you've held, related work experiences.

1. _____

2. _____

3. _____

Education/Training/Relevant Courses/Internships

Record here the kinds of preparation you have had that make you especially suitable for the position.

1. _____

2. _____

3. _____

Competencies

Record here what you do especially well, perhaps classified into categories such as computer skills, communication skills, research skills, or whatever is relevant to the particular position you're seeking.

1. _____

2. _____

3. _____

Questions to Ask

Record here any questions you want to ask about the position or about when decisions will be made.

1. _____

2. _____

3. _____

Next Step?

Ask about the next step and be sure to record what you have to do. Do this during the interview; don't risk forgetting it.

1. _____

2. _____

3. _____

Thank the Interviewer!

3. Dress professionally. Even though the interviewer won't see you (unless this is a video conference), you'll probably act more professionally if you are dressed professionally (at least to some

extent). Avoid doing the phone interview in your pajamas which may lead you to act in a more relaxed and informal manner than you might want. Some interview experts recommend that you stand up during the call; it will help you sound more professional than you might while sitting in a recliner.

4. Thank the interviewer for making time for the phone call. Of course, it's the interviewer's job to make these calls, but thank the person anyway.

5. Speak professionally and dynamically. Avoid peppering your talk with expressions you might use with friends on the phone—"like," "you know," or "I mean." Avoid interrupting the interviewer even if you're absolutely sure you know what he or she is going to say next. Use the interviewer's title plus last name, unless you're asked to use just a first name.

6. Throughout your conversation, pause enough so that the interviewer can interject comments but not so long or so frequently as to make yourself seem uncertain.

7. Give verbal feedback during the call that tells the interviewer you're following and understanding what is being said. These are sometimes called *minimal responses*, such as "I see," "yes," and "I understand."

8. Pay particular attention to any cues the interviewer gives you that can help you regulate your conversation. Often interviewers will tell you very explicitly what they want: Tell me *briefly* what you did at XYZ. Or, What's the *single* most important factor in a job to you? At other times, the cues will be more subtle—an interjected "OK" that may suggest you cut your response short or move on to the next question.

9. If you're in doubt about anything you feel might be important, seek clarification. This is a lot better than going on and on about a question you weren't asked.

10. Ask about the next step. Remember that the main purpose of the phone interview is to get to the face-to-face interview. Make sure you take accurate notes about the time and location for a second interview should it be set up during the phone interview. Often, you'll be notified by phone call, e-mail, or letter. In any event, make sure you know what the next step is.

11. Thank the interviewer for his or her time, express your enjoyment of the interview (not "This wasn't as hard as I thought it would be" or anything that suggests a less than total command of the phone interview but with something like "I enjoyed learning more about XYZ"), and reiterate your interest in the job and in working at XYZ.

12. Follow up the interview by (1) keeping a log of the major issues covered, the name of the interviewer, and especially what the next step is, and (2) writing a thank-you note in e-mail or by regular post.

INTERVIEWING CHOICE POINT During a phone interview, the interviewer makes some remarks you find ethnocentric and culturally offensive, saying "I'm pleased you're not one of them." *What options do you have at this point? What are the main advantages and disadvantages of each option? What would you say?*

Online. Much like the phone interview, the online interview may be used to narrow a large pool of people down to the one, two, or three people who will be invited to a face-to-face interview. Here are a few guidelines to use in the online interview.

1. Follow all the courtesies that you would extend to the interviewer if you were on the phone. Thank the interviewer when beginning the e-mail exchange and in the final e-mail.

2. Write your e-mails as if you were writing an English composition that was to be graded. Avoid cute emoticons, acronyms, varied colors, and the general style that you might use in writing on Facebook or MySpace.

3. If the online interview involves video, follow the same principles as for the face-to-face interview. For example, you'd want to dress professionally—though perhaps not in a business suit. And you'd want to make sure that your desk at home is relatively neat; it should project the image you want to communicate.

4. Be brief. Conciseness is valued throughout the business world and especially in interviews.

5. If your online message is a response, make sure you answer all questions. It's also often a good idea to cover yourself by saying

something like, "If you need any additional information or would like me to elaborate on any of these points, please let me know."

6. If an e-mail you receive from the company copied others then hit "Reply All." Otherwise, just use "Reply."

Individual and Group Interviews At times, you may be asked in for a group interview. The group interview takes two basic forms: (1) several interviewers with one applicant, and (2) one interviewer with several applicants.

In the first case, sometimes called a panel interview, several interviewers will interview one candidate. This type of interview is common in interviewing a potential college professor, in which case the entire department or perhaps a departmental committee interviews the applicant. Similarly, a condo board might interview a prospective buyer.

In the second case, an interviewer (often one person but at times there may be several interviewers involved) interviews several candidates at the same time. This type of interview is often a screening interview, designed to narrow down the field and eventually select one, two, or three people for one-on-one interviews. Sometimes, this interview will proceed like a normal interview with questions and answers. At other times, the interviewer may assign the group of applicants an exercise or problem to solve and observe their performance. This provides the organization with insight into the candidates' ability to deal with real work problems and to interact effectively with others. A great example of this occurred in *Men in Black* when the candidates were given forms to complete but no desks on which to write. Only the hero—Will Smith—demonstrated creativity by finding a flat service to write on. Needless to say, Smith got the job.

Although the skills of the one-on-one interview apply here as well, there are a few additional points to keep in mind for the group interview.

First, be positive toward the other applicants. Compliment or complement their ideas but don't criticize them. Your positiveness toward the others will demonstrate your ability to work effectively in teams—a characteristic desired by most large corporations. Likewise, be positive toward the interviewers, your previous employers, and this new company that you hope to be working for shortly. And demonstrate this positiveness both verbally (say positive things) and nonverbally (for example, lean forward to demonstrate your interest rather than leaning backward, which may indicate a lack of interest or a superior attitude).

Second, remember that your task here is to distinguish yourself from the others while at the same time working effectively with them. Generally, it's better to:

- demonstrate the ability to lead rather than to follow, although being an effective team member is also essential

- participate actively rather than passively, but not to the point of dominating or interrupting others

- contribute original ideas rather than just reacting to the ideas of others, although reacting to the ideas of others (positively) is also important

- demonstrate comfort with the situation, but not to the point of being overly relaxed or over confident

INTERVIEWING CHOICE POINT In a group interview, you find that all seven of the other interviewees are of the same race and gender and you're the different one. During the interview, the interviewer asks each person to explain how he or she is feeling right now. You wonder if you should mention this race–gender difference. *What are your options for responding to this question?* What would you say?

Third, thank the interviewer—usually at the beginning of the interview ("Thanks for having me in to interview at XYZ"), at the end ("I appreciated the opportunity to meet with you"), and in a follow-up note, again thanking the interviewer and reiterating your interest in the company and perhaps your great fit with the company ("It was a pleasure interviewing with XYZ; it sounds like a great opportunity and one for which I feel qualified both in terms of experience and interest").

Fourth, ask relevant questions that show your knowledge of the company and of the particular job. To do this effectively, you'll have to do some homework and research the company, the position, and, if possible, the interviewers. Generally, assertiveness will be appreciated—unless it veers off into aggressiveness or seems arrogant.

Fifth, maintain eye contact with the interviewers and with the other candidates. Focus your eye contact on the speaker. If one member of a panel asks you a question, focus your eye contact on that person as you begin your answer, then look at other members of the panel as you continue your answer, and then return your focus to the questioner as you complete your answer.

Types of Interview Questions

As already stated, the uniqueness of the interview is that it takes place in question-and-answer format. Consequently, understanding the different types of questions may help you ask questions more effectively (in an information-gathering interview) and respond to questions more effectively (in an employment interview). Questions may be analyzed in terms of at least the following dimensions:

- neutral–leading

- open–closed

- primary–follow-up

- direct–indirect

As you read this section, recognize that asking questions is not the only way to elicit information from an interviewee. For example, after a question has been asked, you might paraphrase it (if you want the interviewee to expand on what she or he just said) or you might use minimal responses ("I see," "right") that encourage the interviewee to elaborate. And of course as an interviewer, you can always ask for more information ("That sounds interesting; tell me more").

Neutral–Leading Questions **Neutral questions** and their opposite, **leading questions,** refer to the extent to which the question reveals the answer the interviewer wants from the interviewee. Some questions are neutral and don't specify any answer as more appropriate than any other. At the other extreme are questions that are leading, or loaded. These clearly indicate the answer the interviewer expects or wants. Compare the following questions:

- How did you feel about managing your own web design firm?

- You must really enjoy managing your own web design company, don't you?

The first question is neutral and allows you to respond in any way; it asks for no particular answer. The second question is biased; it specifies that the interviewer expects a "yes." Between the neutrality of "How did you feel about your previous job?" and the bias of "You must have loved your previous job, didn't you?" there are questions that specify with varying degrees of strength the answer the interviewer expects or prefers. For example:

- Did you like your previous job?

- Did you dislike your previous job very much?

- It seems like it would be an interesting job, no?

An interviewer who asks too many biased questions will not learn about the interviewee's talents or experiences, but only about the interviewee's ability to give the desired answer. As an interviewee, pay special attention to any biases in the question. Don't give the responses your interviewer expects if they're not what you believe to be correct or know to be true. This would be unethical. However, when your responses are not what the interviewer expects, consider explaining why you're responding as you are. For example, to the biased question, "It seems like it would be an interesting job, no?" you might respond: "It was interesting most of the time, but I'm looking for a position that allows for greater creativity."

Sometimes an interviewer will ask a question that is designed to provoke defensiveness to see how you'll react to criticism, for example, "Do you think you're really qualified for this position? It requires a high level of dedication and commitment" or "Don't you think you're asking for a lot of money for an entry level position?" The trick is to treat these questions like any others—logically, positively, and without any visible signs of defensiveness.

> **INTERVIEWING CHOICE POINT** An interviewer tries to provoke defensiveness by asking you, "Why did you go to such a poorly rated college? Do you think they prepared you for a job like this?" *What are some ways you can deal with this? What would you say?*

Open–Closed Questions   Openness refers to the degree of freedom you have to respond, both in content and format. At times there's almost unlimited latitude in what may constitute an answer to **open-ended questions,** for example, "What do you like to do most of all?" or "Why do you want to work at Peabody and Peabody?" At the opposite extreme are **closed questions** that require only a "yes" or "no," for example, "Are you willing to relocate to San Francisco?" and "Can you work with electronic spreadsheets?" Between these extremes are short-answer questions, those that are relatively closed and to which you have only limited freedom in responding, for example, "What would you do as manager here?" or "What computer skills do you have?" Part of the art of successful interviewing is to respond with answers that are appropriate to the question's level of openness. Thus if you're asked a question like "Why do you want to work at Peabody and Peabody?" you're expected to speak at some length. If you're asked, "Are you willing to relocate to San Francisco?" then a simple "yes" or "no" (with or without a qualification) will suffice, for example, "Absolutely, though it would take me about six weeks to close my affairs here in Boston."

Primary–Follow-Up Questions   **Primary questions** introduce a topic and are often relatively general ("What did you study in college?"). **Follow-up questions** ask for elaboration on what was just said ("I majored in economics too. What did you hate most about studying economics?"). Too many primary questions and not enough follow-up questions may communicate a lack of interest and perhaps a failure to listen as effectively as possible. For example, if you're interviewing a scientist and ask only primary questions, it will easily appear as though you're just following a script and are not really prepared for the interview. Follow-up questions that ask for clarification, elaboration, or illustrations are essential to getting worthwhile information. A balance between primary and follow-up questions, determined in large part by the situation and by your own communication goals, is best.

Direct–Indirect Questions Questions of these types will vary greatly from one culture to another. In the United States, be prepared for rather direct questions, whether you're being interviewed for information or for a job. In Japan, on the other hand, the interviewee is expected to reveal herself or himself despite the indirectness of the questions.

Similarly, cultures vary in what they consider appropriate directness in speaking of one's accomplishments, say, in a job interview. In many Asian cultures, the interviewee is expected to appear modest and unassuming and should allow his or her competences to emerge indirectly during the interview. In the United States, on the other hand, you're expected to state your competences without excessive modesty. In fact, many interviewers expect a certain amount of hyperbole and exaggeration, but not to the point of being dishonest.

INTERVIEWING EXERCISE
Classifying Types of Questions

Classify the following questions in terms of their being neutral or leading, open or closed, primary or follow-up, and direct or indirect. Note, of course, that any one question may be classified into several categories. That is, a question may be both leading and open or may be neutral, open, primary, and direct. Understanding the type of question will help you in determining the most effective types of responses.

1. What made you select the University of Rhode Island?
2. What did you think of your education at URI?
3. You said salary was not your most important consideration; what is?
4. What made you want to be an accountant?
5. I assume you'll be comfortable working in teams. Yes?
6. What would be your ideal work situation?
7. Would you be available to start in September?
8. How do you see your career 10 years from now?
9. You must have received great training while working at ABCD, no?
10. What salary range are you looking at?

Effective Interpersonal Communication

Regardless of the type of interview in which you find yourself, you'll need to apply the skills of interpersonal communication, avoid the common mistakes, and be prepared to identify your own communication competences.

Interpersonal Communication Skills   Here, for example, are some of the major skills of interpersonal communication applied to an interviewing context.

- *Openness.* Take an active role in the interview. Initiate topics or questions when appropriate. Avoid appearing as a passive participant, waiting for a stimulus. In the employment interview, answer all questions asked fully and directly. Avoid one-word answers that may signal a lack of interest or knowledge. Avoid appearing to be hiding something.

- *Positiveness.* Express positive interest in the person you're interviewing or in the position for which you're applying. Avoid statements that are critical of the person you're interviewing; this may well end the interview. In the employment interview, avoid statements that are critical of yourself and others. Demonstrate positiveness and respect for the interview process, the interviewer, and the company. And express positiveness for your previous employment experiences. Never bad-mouth your former employers. If you do, you may be seen as a negative person or as one who will later bad-mouth the company at which you're now applying for a job. Emphasize your positive qualities.

- **Immediacy.** Connect with the person you're interviewing or with the interviewer *throughout the interview*, for example, by using the person's name, focusing clearly on the individual's remarks, and expressing responsibility for your thoughts and feelings. Maintain eye contact; people who avoid eye contact are often judged to be ill at ease, as though they're afraid to engage in meaningful interaction.

- **Interaction Management.** Ensure the other person's satisfaction by being positive, complimentary, and generally cooperative. And be brief but not overly brief. If you make a mistake, admit it. Attempting to cover up obvious mistakes communicates a lack of confidence. Only a confident person can openly admit her or his mistakes and not worry about what others will think.

- **Expressiveness.** Let your nonverbal behaviors (especially facial expression) and vocal variety reflect your verbal messages and your general enthusiasm and high energy (but not too high). Avoid fidgeting and excessive moving about. Vary your vocal rate, pitch, and pausing, for example, to best reflect your meanings (DeGroot & Motowidlo, 1999). Avoid excessive movements, especially self-touching. Tapping a pencil, crossing and uncrossing your legs in rapid succession, and touching your face or hair all communicate uneasiness and a lack of social confidence. Avoid vocalized pauses—the *ers* and *ahs* that frequently punctuate conversations and communicate hesitation or an uncertainty about what to say. Similarly, avoid peppering your speech with "like," "you know" or "I mean" interjections.

- **Other-Orientation.** Focus on the person you're interviewing or on the interviewer and on the company. Express agreement and ask for clarification as appropriate. But, at least in the employment interview, don't ask for agreement from the interviewer by using tag questions, for example, "That was appropriate, don't you think?" or by saying normally declarative sentences with a rising intonation, thereby turning them into questions, for example, "I'll arrive at nine?" Asking for agreement communicates a lack of confidence in making decisions and in expressing opinions. See the questions from the asker's point of view. Focus your eye contact and orient your body toward the interviewer. Lean forward as appropriate.

- **Cultural Sensitivity.** Express your cultural sensitivity by, for example, using the appropriate and preferred terms for different cultural groups. Avoid any negative reaction to members of other groups; you never know how the person you're interviewing or the interviewer feels about these things. Cultural sensitivity alone will likely not get you the job, but insensitivity will almost surely rule you out.

- **Flexibility.** Demonstrate your flexibility, whether by shifting from one topic to another as the person you're interviewing does or dealing with hypothetical workplace issues to which you may be asked to respond.

- **Confidence.** Demonstrate your confidence but without immodesty and certainly without any hint of arrogance. Appear as if you are equal to the task, regardless of what that task may be. And, in the event that you are simply not competent in

INTERVIEWING CHOICE POINT The job interviewer belittles your experience, which you thought was your strong point. Several times during the interview comments were made that your experiences were "in school" or "with only a few people." You think your experience has more than prepared you for this job and you want to make sure the interviewer knows this. *What options do you have for responding? What do you say?*

a given area, admit it and add that you feel quite confident that you can learn whatever it is you don't know now (assuming you feel you can and will).

Common Interpersonal Mistakes   In addition to demonstrating the qualities of interpersonal effectiveness, avoid behaviors that create negative impressions during employment interviews. Here are a few of the most common mistakes that interviewees make:

- Being unprepared; they forget to bring their résumé or don't show that they know anything about the company.

- Demonstrating poor communication skills; they avoid looking at the interviewer, slouch, slur their words, speak in an overly low or too-rapid voice, give one-word answers, fidget, play with their pens or résumés, dress inappropriately, or talk without knowing when enough is enough.

- Appearing to have an unpleasant personality; they appear defensive, cocky, lacking in assertiveness, extremely introverted, or overly aggressive.

- Showing little initiative; they fail to pick up on ramifications of the interviewer's questions, give one-word answers, and don't ask questions when appropriate.

- Listening ineffectively; they are easily distracted, need to have questions repeated, or fail to maintain appropriate eye contact.

- Being late for an appointment; this tells the interviewer that they may be late for work as well.

▼ | ONLINE HELP

Here are a few helpful websites that discuss interviewing mistakes, in addition to providing a great deal of interviewing advice on other issues: www.careerbuilder.com/Custom/MSN/CareerAdvice, www.Careerbuilder.co.uk/UK/JobSeeker/CareerAdvice, www.worktree.com/tbIN_mistakes.cfm, www.allbusiness.com, and http://career-advice.monster.com/interview-tips.

Communication Skill Set   In addition to demonstrating the skills of interpersonal communication and avoiding major mistakes during the interview, you'll often be asked about your own communication skills. Because of this, it may prove helpful to complete the accompanying Communication Skill Set worksheet.

COMMUNICATION SKILL SET

Identify the communication skills you might want to emphasize during a job interview. Use the classification system proposed here or develop your own, depending on the nature of the job for which you're interviewing. Examples are provided in italics.

Interpersonal Skills
[For example, responsiveness to feedback: *One of the things I always do is to listen very carefully to feedback, especially negative feedback. I make it my business to know what users think of our products.*]

1. _____

2. _____

3. _____

Team Member Skills
[For example, perspective taking: *I think one of my team skills is to look at issues from a variety of points of view, rather than just the one or two obvious sides.*]

1. _____

2. _____

3. _____

Team Leadership Skills
[For example, openness and supportiveness: *I make sure the members of the group each get a fair chance to express their points of view in a supportive atmosphere and without fear of criticism.*]

1. _____

2. _____

3. _____

Presentation Skills

[For example, competence in presentation media: *I took a course in public speaking where we had to use PowerPoint in all of our speeches and I've since used it in all my oral presentations in other courses and later at ABCD. I also feel comfortable using transparencies, video, flip charts, graphs, and just about any presentation media.*]

1. _____

2. _____

3. _____

Ethical Considerations in Interviewing

In both the information and the employment interview, there are ethical principles that should be followed. Here, in brief, are some such principles (www.studentaffairs.cmu.edu and www.tcnj.edu/~career/ guidance, both accessed November 20, 2008).

The Information Interview

- Be on time for any interview as scheduled. Time is valuable, especially for anyone worthy of being interviewed. It also shows that you respect the person's time and willingness to sit for the interview and may be helpful in establishing rapport.

- Respect the person's confidentiality when something is said "off the record." While it may be tempting to repeat things shared off the record—they're often the juiciest—resist such impulses. It can easily backfire and create problems for you.

- Obtain permission both to use the information you get in your interview and for how it will be used. If you're going to use the information for a term paper or for an article in the college newspaper, then get permission from the interviewee for this specific use. It would be unethical to use it elsewhere if the agreement was to use it only in, say, a term paper.

■ Don't misrepresent, slant, or quote the person out of context. Your objective should be to present the information given during the interview as fairly as possible.

The Employment Interview

■ Attend all interviews you schedule on time. This is not only ethical (after all, it's unfair to waste people's time) but also effective interviewing technique.

■ Present yourself—your experience, your skills—truthfully. Your résumé and your discussions during the interview should be truthful. If, for example, you're asked about your knowledge of PowerPoint and you've only used it once, then say so. But, you can also add that you intend to learn more about it (assuming that you do).

■ Honor all agreements you make during the interview, for example, to attend a second interview or to send follow-up materials. In addition to being ethical, this will also show your commitment to agreements in general, a valued organizational quality.

■ Stop interviewing after you've accepted a job offer. It's unethical to interview for a job you aren't interested in accepting. Cancel any scheduled interviews once you accept a position.

Unit 2

The Information Interview

In the **information interview,** the interviewer tries to learn something about the interviewee. Variations on the basic information interview would include, for example (Powell & Amsbary, 2006):

- journalistic interviews in which a journalist interviews news-makers and then communicates this back to a large audience

- medical interviews in which a health professional seeks to learn a person's medical history

- oral history interviews of people who have witnessed important events as a way of writing history from the perspective of those who lived it; younger family members increasingly are interviewing older members as a way of recording their family history

- police interrogations in which law enforcement personnel question witnesses or supposed law breakers in an effort to find out what really happened

- research interviews in which you interview someone at the company you want to join or a professional in your field to get some inside information on what the company is looking for or on what it's like working in the field (see Unit 3)

▼ ONLINE HELP

Take a look at The Journalist's Toolbox (http://www.americanpressinstitute .org/content/4056.cfm). It contains a wealth of materials useful to the information interviewer.

In the information interview—unlike the employment interview—the person interviewed is usually an individual of some reputation and accomplishment. The interviewer asks a series of questions designed to elicit the interviewee's views, beliefs, insights, perspectives, predictions, life history, and so on. Examples of the information interview include those published in popular magazines; TV interviews conducted by David Letterman, Katie Couric, and Barbara Walters; and those a lawyer conducts during a trial. All aim to elicit specific information from someone who supposedly knows something others don't know. Some of these interviews are informative on the surface but persuasive in their main intent. For example, when a singer, writer, or actor comes on a talk show it is usually to sell something—a CD, a book, a recent film or television series.

This discussion concentrates on your role as the interviewer, because that is the role in which you're likely to find yourself serving now and in the near future. Let's say that your interview is designed to get information about a particular field, for example, web design. You want to know about the available job opportunities and the preparation you would need to get into this field. Here are a few guidelines for conducting such information-gathering interviews.

Select the Person

There are several ways to find a likely person to interview. Let's say that you wish to learn something about web publishing. You might, for example, look through your college catalog; there you find that a course on this general topic is offered by Professor Bernard Brommel. You think it might be worthwhile to interview him. Or you visit a variety of newsgroups and discover that

> *To question a wise person is the beginning of wisdom.*
> —GERMAN PROVERB

one particular person has posted extremely well-reasoned articles and you'd like to interview her to get her opinion on web design and advice on how you might break into this field. If you want to contact a book author, you can always write to the author in care of the publisher or editor (listed on the copyright page), although many authors are now including their e-mail address. You can often find the address and phone number of most professional people by calling the appropriate professional association for a directory listing (the *Encyclopedia of Associations* lists nearly every professional association in the country). Or you can write to the person via the association's website. Newsgroup and listserv writers are the easiest to contact because their e-mail addresses are included with their posts. It's often helpful to interview someone from the company you hope to join. Someone at a job fair or the personnel officer at the company should be able to help you locate an appropriate interviewee.

After you've selected one of the people you hope to interview, but before you pursue the interview, try to learn something about this person. Consult an online library or bookstore to see if this person has written a book, or go through a CD-ROM database to see if this person has written any research articles. Search through the databases covering computers, the Internet, and the World Wide Web. Search the Web and Usenet groups to see if the person has a web page or posts to newsgroups. You may find that the person encourages people to correspond via e-mail.

Secure an Appointment

Phone the person or send a letter or e-mail requesting an interview. In your call or letter, identify the purpose of your request and state

---

▼ **ONLINE HELP**

You can often find experts through a variety of websites, for example, www.experts.com and http://www.usc.edu/dept/news_service/ experts_directory.html.

that you would like a brief interview. For example, you might say: "I'm preparing for a career in web design and I would appreciate it if I could interview you to learn more about the subject. The interview would take about 15 minutes." (It's helpful to let the person know it will not take too long; she or he is more likely to agree to being interviewed.) Generally, it's best to be available at the interviewee's convenience. So indicate flexibility on your part, for example, "I can interview you any afternoon this week."

You may find it necessary to conduct the interview by phone. In this case, call to set up a time for a future interview call. For example, you might say, "I'm interested in a career in web design and I would like to interview you on the job opportunities in this field. If you agree, I can call you back at a time that's convenient for you." In this way, you don't run the risk of asking the person to participate in an interview while eating lunch, talking with colleagues, or running to class.

Prepare Your Questions

Preparing questions ahead of time will ensure that you use the time available to your best advantage. Of course, as the interview progresses, other questions will come to mind and should be asked. But having a prepared list of questions will help you obtain the information you need most easily.

In a job research interview you might seek to find answers to such questions as: *What in your background and experience would be useful to mention? What do you need to know about the company and the specific position that will help you interview effectively?* And, of course, *What do you have to do to secure an interview?*

Do be careful, however, that you don't read your questions. Much as you would lose spontaneity if you read a public speech, you lose spontaneity if you read your questions. So perhaps after writing your list of questions, you might want to create a reminder list consisting of only key words and phrases. If you practice with this list, you'll be likely to cover all the important questions you want to ask and at the same time communicate in a conversational style.

Establish Rapport

Open the interview with an expression of thanks for making the time available to you. Many people receive lots of requests and it helps if you also remind the person of your specific purpose. You might say something like: "I really appreciate your making time for this interview. As I mentioned, I'm preparing a speech on the job opportunities in web design and your expertise and experience in this area will help a great deal."

> **▤ INTERVIEWING CHOICE POINT** You finally got the opportunity to interview on the campus radio station a famous author who is notorious for being difficult. You need to establish rapport right at the start of the interview. *What are some options for establishing this needed rapport? What do you say?*

After you've established rapport, ask your first question. On the basis of the answers to your first few questions—their length and tone—you'll be able to judge the kinds of questions that will work best and how you can use follow-up questions to get more detail.

Tape the Interview

Generally, it's a good idea to tape the interview. This gives you a more complete record of the interview, which you'll be able to review as you need to. It will also free you to concentrate on the interview rather than on trying to write down the person's responses. But ask permission first. Some people prefer not to have informal interviews taped. Even if the interview is being conducted by phone, ask permission if you intend to tape the conversation.

Taping the job research interview will ensure that you have the specific information you need to follow up. If you don't record the interview, make sure you write down any important names, addresses, phone numbers, or dates.

Ask Open-Ended Questions

Use questions that provide the person you're interviewing with room to discuss the issues you want to raise. Thus, instead of asking "Do you have formal training in web publishing?" (a question that requires a simple "yes" or "no" and will not be very informative), you might ask, "Can you tell me something about your background in this field?" (an open-ended question that allows the person greater freedom in responding). In the job research interview, you might ask the open-ended question, "How should I dress for the job interview?" rather than the closed-ended question, "Should I wear a suit?" You can then ask follow-up questions to pursue more specifically the topics raised in the answers to your open-ended questions.

Close and Follow Up the Interview

At the end of the interview, thank the person for making the time to speak with you, for being informative, cooperative, helpful, or whatever. Showing your appreciation will make it a lot easier if you want to return for a second interview. Within the next two or three days, follow up the interview with a brief note of thanks that expresses your appreciation for the time given you, your enjoyment in speaking with the person, and your pleasure in accomplishing your goal of getting the information you needed. Figure 2.1 on page 33 shows a sample letter. A worksheet to help you prepare for your information interview follows on page 34.

INTERVIEWING CHOICE POINT You're interviewing an 80-year-old writer about romantic affairs with famous movie stars. But, instead of being forthright, as you anticipated, your interviewee expresses embarrassment at speaking of these relationships with such a young interviewer as you. This part of the writer's life is crucial to the magazine for which you're writing the interview. *What are some options you have for convincing this writer to open up? What do you say?*

Practicing Interviewing Skills

Form three-person groups, preferably among persons who don't know each other well or who have had relatively little interaction. Designate one person as the interviewer, another as the interviewee, and the third as the interview analyst. The interview analyst should choose one of the following situations:

1. An interview for the position of camp counselor for children with disabilities
2. An interview for a part in a new Broadway musical
3. A therapy interview to focus on communication problems in relating to superiors
4. A job research interview in which an accounting major interviews an accountant at XYZ to obtain information that will be helpful in the actual job interview
5. An interview between the chair of the communication department and a candidate for the position of instructor of human communication

After the situation is chosen, the interviewer should interview the interviewee for approximately 10 minutes. The analyst should observe but not interfere in any way. After the interview is over, the analyst should offer a detailed analysis, considering each of the following:

1. What happened during the interview (essentially a description of the interaction)?
2. What was handled well?
3. What went wrong? What aspects of the interview were not handled as effectively as they might have been?
4. What could have been done to make the interview more effective?

The analyst for each interview may then report the major findings to the whole class. The group may then develop a list of "common faults" or "suggestions for improving interviews."

123 Walnut Street (Apt. 3C)
New York, New York 10038-1525
September 30, 2010

Ms. Anita Brice
Brice Publishers, Inc.
17 Michigan Avenue (Suite 233)
Chicago, Illinois 60600-2345

Dear Ms. Brice:

    It was a pleasure meeting you on Tuesday. Thanks for taking the time to talk to me. I greatly appreciate your sharing your knowledge of the desktop publishing industry as well as your insights into the future of this business.

    I now have a much more complete understanding of the field. Understanding your background and experience has also given me a clear idea of the kinds of skills I'll need to succeed in this growing industry.

    Again, thank you for your time and your willingness to share your expertise. I wish you continued success.

Sincerely,

Carlos Villas

Carlos Villas

Figure 2.1
A Sample Letter of Thanks for an Information Interview

INFORMATION INTERVIEW PREPARATION GUIDE

Here are a few questions that will help you plan for the information interview. The questions are designed to help you focus the interview and to anticipate any possible problem areas. This added preparation will also help to reduce any apprehension and give you a greater sense of control over the interview process.

1. **Opening.** How will you open the interview? List one, two, or three things you might say in opening the interview that go beyond the simple "Thank you for agreeing to be interviewed." Next, identify what purpose you hope to accomplish with each opening statement.

Opening Statement

1. _____
   _____
   _____
   _____
   _____

2. _____
   _____
   _____
   _____
   _____

3. _____
   _____
   _____
   _____
   _____

Opening Statement Purpose

1. _____
   _____
   _____
   _____
   _____

2. _____
   _____
   _____
   _____
   _____

3. _____
   _____
   _____
   _____
   _____

2. **Goals.** List two or three goals you want to accomplish in the interview and the strategies you'd use to accomplish these goals.

General Interview Goals	Strategies for Accomplishing Your Goals
1. _____	1. _____
2. _____	2. _____
3. _____	3. _____

3. **Questions.** What questions do you want to ask? List five major questions that you want to ask. For each question, consider the interviewee's anticipated response, and identify at least one possible follow-up question.

Major Questions	Follow-Up Questions
1. _____	1. _____
_____	_____
_____	_____
_____	_____
_____	_____
_____	_____
_____	_____
_____	_____
2. _____	2. _____
_____	_____
_____	_____
_____	_____
_____	_____
_____	_____
_____	_____
_____	_____
3. _____	3. _____
_____	_____
_____	_____
_____	_____
_____	_____
_____	_____
_____	_____

4. **Closing.** How will you close the interview? List two or three goals you want to accomplish in closing the interview and what, specifically, you'll say to accomplish these goals.

Closing Goals

1. _____

2. _____

3. _____

Communicating the Goals

1. _____

2. _____

3. _____

5. **Problems.** What possible problems might arise as you conduct this information interview? List two or three possible problems and what you'd do if they did occur.

Possible Problems

1. _____

2. _____

3. _____

Possible Ways to Handle the Problems

1. _____

2. _____

3. _____

6. **Follow-Up.** How will you follow up the interview? Write a paragraph of what you'd say in a phone, e-mail, or letter follow-up.

_____

_____

_____

_____

_____

_____

_____

_____

_____

_____

_____

_____

_____

_____

_____

_____

_____

_____

_____

_____

_____

_____

_____

_____

_____

_____

_____

_____

_____

The Employment Interview

Perhaps of most concern to college students is the **employment interview**. In this type of interview, a great deal of information and persuasion will be exchanged. The interviewer will learn about you, your interests, your talents—and, if clever enough, some of your weaknesses and liabilities. In turn, you'll be informed about the nature of the company, its benefits, its advantages—and, if you're clever enough, some of its disadvantages and problems. The interviewer may persuade you of the benefits of working for the company and you'll persuade the interviewer that you're the right person for the job. Supplement the discussion here with materials available on the various websites included in this unit.

Today, the employment interview is likely to be an important part of your professional life, beyond getting your initial job. You'll likely interview for jobs throughout your professional life. And even when you stay with the same company, you're likely to interview for promotions and different positions. In addition, you're likely to

---

▼ ONLINE HELP

Many colleges and universities maintain extensive open websites devoted to employment interviewing. For example, the School of Business at the University of Wisconsin, Madison, maintains an online career center that provides numerous aids for effective job interviewing, including a sample mock interview video (www.bus.wisc.edu/career). The University of South Carolina at Spartanburg (www.uscs.edu/student_life/career_center) and the University of Dayton (http://careers/udayton.edu) also have excellent and practical websites to help prepare you further for that important job interview.

Figure 3.1
Indiana University Southeast Website (www.ius.edu/careerservices/article/interviewing)

College websites are probably the most useful when it comes to locating helpful material on interviewing. Most such websites are open to everyone and can be accessed easily through your favorite search engine. Also see the websites from Indiana University School of Law (http://indylaw.indiana.edu/career/interviewing) and Radford University's Informational Interviewing Guide (http://72.14.205.104/search?q).

Courtesy of Indiana University Southeast Career Services Office. Copyright © 2004 Indiana University Trustees.

participate in other kinds of workplace interviews once you do get the job:

- In the **appraisal interview,** management or more experienced colleagues assess the interviewee's performance. The general aim is to discover what the interviewee is doing well (and to praise this) and not doing well and why (and to suggest ways to improve). These interviews are important because they help new members of an organization see how their performance matches up with the expectations of those making promotion and firing decisions. They make clear what you'll need to do to advance in the organization and perhaps how you might go about it.

- In the **top-grading interview,** management attempts to select only A-level candidates. This type of interview, a relatively new addition to the employment interview, is extremely intense, as compared with the typical employment interview, and seeks to get an in-depth, detailed picture of the candidate. Here, the candidate's entire job history is carefully reviewed and information about each of the candidate's successes and failures is secured and analyzed. The overall objective here is to get the best candidates possible and to eliminate those who are not among the best.

- In the **exit interview,** used widely by organizations in the United States and throughout the world, management tries to discover why an employee is leaving the company. Because all organizations compete in one way or another for superior workers, when an employee leaves a company voluntarily, it's important to know why, to prevent other valuable workers from leaving as well. When the employee is not leaving voluntarily, this exit interview functions to provide a way of making the exit as pleasant and as efficient as possible for both employee and employer.

Prepare Yourself

Before going into a job interview, prepare yourself. One way to do this is through general long-term preparation, especially networking, and the second way is to do your homework for the specific interview.

Network   Networking is especially important in finding a job and, in the popular mind, is often viewed as having this one major function. Actually networking is a much broader process that can be viewed as one of using other people's suggestions and experiences to help you solve a problem or at least offer insights that bear on your problem—for example, how to publish your manuscript, where to look for low-cost auto insurance, how to find an affordable apartment, or how to empty your cache.

Networking has at least two forms: informal and formal. Informal networking is what we do every day when we find ourselves in a new situation or unable to answer questions. Thus, for example, if you're new at a school, you might ask someone in your class where's the best place to eat or shop for new clothes or who's the best teacher for interpersonal communication. In the same way, when you enter a new work environment, you might ask more experienced workers how to perform certain tasks or who to avoid or approach when you have questions.

Formal networking is the same, except that it's a lot more systematic and strategic. It's the establishment of connections with people who can help you by answering questions, getting you a job, helping you get promoted, or helping you relocate or accomplish any task you want to accomplish.

At the most obvious level, you can network with people you already know. If you review the list of people in your acquaintance, you'll probably

> **INTERVIEWING CHOICE POINT** One of your colleagues has taken networking to its ugliest extreme and asks everyone for information without ever once trying to find it on his own. Today he comes to you for a phone number that he can easily find in his own directory. You're fed up. *What are some ways you have for confronting this abuse of your time? What would you say?*

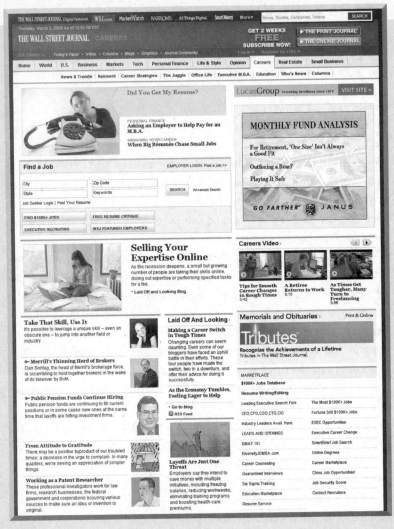

Figure 3.2

Career Journal (www.careerjournal.com)

CareerJournal.com, maintained by the *Wall Street Journal*, one of the premier financial newspapers, contains all sorts of professional and career advice. The material on interviewing is current, well-written, and extremely practical.

Reprinted with permission of the *Wall Street Journal*, Copyright © 2009 Dow Jones & Company, Inc. All Rights Reserved Worldwide.

discover that you know a great number of people with very specialized knowledge who can be of assistance to you in a wide variety of ways. In some cultures (Brazil is one example), friendships are established in part because of the potential networking connections that a particular person has (Rector & Neiva, 1996). You can also network with people who know people you know. Thus you may contact a friend's friend to find out if the firm she or he works for is hiring. Or you may contact people you have no connection with. Perhaps you've read something the person wrote or you've heard the person's name raised in connection with an area you're interested in and you want to get more information. With e-mail addresses so readily available, it's now common to e-mail individuals who have particular expertise and ask them questions.

In college you have a variety of networking opportunities. In fact, one of the great values of college is that it provides a wide variety of opportunities for networking now and throughout your professional career. The clubs you belong to will often invite prominent speakers (who may well be influential in companies you may want to join). The internships that many academic departments encourage students to enter will often present a wide variety of networking possibilities—from assistants who can tell you when openings will be available to management personnel who might offer advice, employment leads, and recommendations. Working in community-based programs—another initiative in many colleges—will likewise offer networking opportunities.

The great value of networking, of course, is that it provides you with access to a wealth of specialized information. At the same time, it often makes accessing that information a lot easier than if you had to find it by yourself.

▼ ONLINE HELP

Take the interviewing quiz "Are you ready for your next interview?" offered by UCLA's Career Center (http://career.UCLA.edu/jobsrch/interview/). It will provide another way of preparing for the actual interview.

In networking, it's often recommended that you try to establish relationships that are mutually beneficial. After all, much as others are useful sources of information for you, you're likely to be a useful source of information for others. If you can provide others with helpful information, it's more likely that they will provide helpful information to you. In this way, a mutually satisfying and productive network is established.

Some networking experts advise you to develop files and directories of potentially useful sources that you can contact for needed information. For example, if you're a freelance artist, you might develop a list of persons who might be in a position to offer you work or who might lead you to others who might offer such work. Authors, editors, art directors, administrative assistants, people in advertising, and a host of others might eventually provide useful leads for such work. Creating a directory of such people and keeping in contact with them on a fairly regular basis can often simplify your obtaining freelance work.

Formal networking requires that you take an active part in locating and establishing connections. Be proactive; initiate contacts rather than wait for them to come to you. Of course, this can be overdone; you don't want to rely on other people to do the work you can easily do yourself. And yet, if you're also willing to help others, there is nothing wrong in asking these same people to help you. If you're respectful of their time and expertise, it's likely that your networking attempts will be successful. Following up your requests with thank-you notes, for example, will help you establish networks that can be ongoing productive relationships rather than one-shot affairs.

Most people who fail to get the job they really want fail not because they are not qualified but because they failed in the interview. And most failure occurs because they aren't prepared.
—DAVID W. CRAWLEY, JR.

Homework Interviewing experts suggest that doing your homework consists of researching the field, the position, the company, and current events (Taub, 1997), and by conducting an information interview.

First, research the career field you're entering and its current trends. With this information you'll be able to demonstrate that you're up-to-date and committed to the area you want this company to pay you to work in.

Second, research the specific position you're applying for so you'll be able to show how your skills and talents mesh with the position. You can do this by visiting the company's website and by **job shadowing,** that is, following a person who does essentially what you'd be hired to do. Many schools are now instituting job-shadowing programs to help their students become familiar with specific jobs. Your college's career center will likely have more information on job shadowing.

Also, most large corporations and, increasingly, many small firms, maintain websites and frequently include detailed job descriptions. Prepare yourself to demonstrate your ability to perform each of the tasks noted in the job description. Figure 3.3 on page 48 shows the home page of the Monster Board, which will give you a good starting place in searching websites to learn about jobs and specific companies and even to improve your résumé.

Third, research the company or organization—its history, mission, and current directions. If it's a publishing company, familiarize yourself with their books and software products. If it's an advertising agency, familiarize yourself with their major clients and major advertising campaigns. A good way to do this is to call and ask the company to send you any company brochures, newsletters, or perhaps a quarterly or annual report. And be sure to visit their website; not only will this provide you with lots of useful information about the company, but it will also show the interviewer that you make use of the latest technology. With extensive knowledge of the company, you'll

---

▼ **ONLINE HELP**

Read more about job shadowing. The Wake Country Public School System website explains job shadowing in education (www.wcpss.net/school_to_career/work_based_learning/job_shadow/). Also see JobWeb.com, which contains information on job shadowing and other topics relevant to the job search.

Figure 3.3
Monster Board (www.monster.com)

Monster Board lists thousands of jobs you can access by keyword, location, or industry; it's just one of the many websites that are useful for finding jobs. Take a look at a few others; for example: www.flipdog.com identifies thousands of job opportunities and allows you to post your résumé; www.careerpath.com organizes the classified ads from leading newspapers; and www.jobtrak.com is especially valuable for college students looking for their first job or for internships.
Reprinted with permission of Monster.com.

be able to show your interest and focus on this specific company. One excellent way to do this is to set a news alert on your computer. For example, you can set an alert for the name of the company you're planning to interview with and you'll be sent links to news items in which the name of the company appears. Figure 3.4 is a web screen of Google Alerts, one of several services that allow you to set up these alerts. Of course, you can also use this free service to be alerted to items you're researching for your classes.

Fourth, research what is going on in the world in general and in the business world in particular. This will help you to demonstrate your breadth of knowledge and that you're a well-rounded individual who continues to learn. Reading a good daily newspaper or a weekly news magazine should help you in mastering current events.

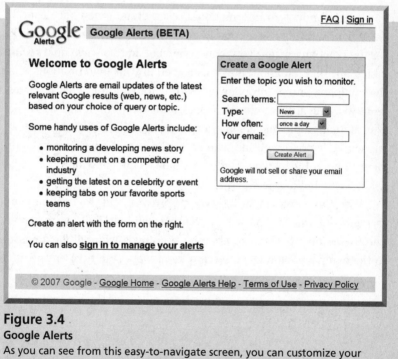

Figure 3.4
Google Alerts
As you can see from this easy-to-navigate screen, you can customize your alerts in several ways with just a few mouse clicks. Also take a look at Yahoo's similar service at http://alerts.yahoo.com.
Screenshot © Google Inc. and is used with permission.

TABLE 3.1 Questions to Ask at the Information Interview

1. What college experiences (courses, extracurricular activities) would XYZ want to see in a successful applicant?

2. What types of entry-level jobs might I be best suited for?

3. What are the best things (worst things) about working at XYZ?

4. What kinds of work would I be doing? For example, would I be working alone or in teams?

5. What are the chances for promotion and advancement?

6. What's a typical day at XYZ like?

7. How can I best secure an interview at XYZ?

8. Do you have any suggestions that would help me in interviewing for a job here at XYZ?

Fifth, conduct an informational research interview (see Unit 2). You might interview someone in your field or someone who works for the company where you're interviewing. In this way you'd secure inside information about how to succeed in your field or about what the company you're interviewing with is looking for, what it values, what working at the company is like, and so on. All of this will make your actual employment interview more likely to result in success, especially if done well in advance of the actual employment interview. Table 3.1 gives you an idea of some of the questions you might ask in such an interview.

With the employment interview, both you and the company are trying to fill a need. You want a job that will help build your career, and the company wants an effective employee who will be an asset to the company. View the interview as an opportunity to engage in a

▼ **ONLINE HELP**

A search for "information interview" will yield lots of useful tips. Two excellent websites are www.quintcareers.com/ information_interview.html and http://hotjobs.yahoo.com/ interview/Mastering_the_Informational_Interview.

joint effort to gain something beneficial. If you approach the interview in this cooperative frame of mind, you are much less likely to become defensive, which in turn will make you a more appealing potential colleague.

Prepare Your Résumé

The most important document you can prepare is your résumé. A **résumé** is a summary of essential information about your experience, education, and abilities. Often, a job applicant submits a résumé in response to a job listing, and if the employer thinks the applicant's résumé is promising, the candidate is invited for an interview. Figure 3.6 on pages 56–57 is a sample résumé that highlights the types of information you need to include in your own résumé.

> *Figure out what your most magnificent qualities are and make them indispensable to the people you want to work with. Notice that I didn't say "work for."*
> —LINDA BLOODWORTH THOMASON

When you are preparing your résumé, consider the advantages of preparing a business card too. Word-processing programs make this easy and inexpensive and, of course, you can change the information with little effort. Try to follow one of the business card templates that comes with your word processor or desktop publishing program. In this way you'll be sure to include the necessary information, omit the nonessential, and present it in a well-designed format.

Types of Résumés   Each occupation seems to prefer a somewhat different résumé, so before preparing your own résumé, investigate the kind of résumés employers in your field prefer and tailor your history and competences to that specific kind of résumé. Amid this diversity, however, there are three main résumé types: chronological, functional, and curriculum vitae.

The Chronological Résumé.   The **chronological résumé** organizes your experience (if possible, in terms of the job titles you've held) beginning with the most recent or current position and working back through your work history. This résumé provides just the right amount of information to be easily and quickly skimmed by the busy personnel manager.

A chronological résumé will work well for you if you have had a continuous history of jobs that can demonstrate your growth—from, say, entry-level positions to ones of greater and greater authority. If you don't have this experience, then this résumé may not work for you right now. It may be the type of résumé you'll write five or ten years from now. A sample chronological résumé appears in Figure 3.5 on page 53.

The Functional Résumé. Whereas the chronological résumé organizes your experience in terms of time units, the **functional résumé** organizes your experience in terms of your competences or skills. Employers like this type of résumé when they can easily identify the competences they are looking for in a new hire in your résumé. If you anticipate that they may not be able to match what they want with what you offer (let's say the job description was somewhat vague and it wasn't clear to you exactly what skills they were looking for), try to describe what you did and perhaps how you did it. This will help the employer see what you might do for them. For example, if you list "bookkeeping" as one of your skills, you might also describe your bookkeeping experience in a bit more detail by saying, for example:

- Maintained the income and expense accounts for a bookstore with sales in excess of $3 million and a staff of 20.

- Supervised college intern bookkeepers for three years.

Figure 3.5
The sample on the next page is from the California State University, Northridge, Career Center (www.csun.edu/career/sampleresumes/sampleresumes_chronol). Also take a look at Louisville University's Résumé, Cover Letter, and Interviewing Tips website at http://louisville.edu/hr/employment/ and Washington College's Résumés & Cover Letters website at http://career.washcoll.edu.interviewing. The University of Alabama maintains a great website with interviewing advice and résumés for just about every field you can imagine (www.uacc.ua.edu/content).

ROBIN A. JOBSEEKER

18013 Future Drive
Northridge, CA 91330

(818)555-2738
Willing to Travel/Relocate

OBJECTIVE	**Pharmaceutical Sales Representative**
EDUCATION	**B.A. Degree—Biology, January 20xx** California State University, Northridge

Science Courses with Laboratories:
- Medical Microbiology
- Human Anatomy
- Medical Mycology
- Cell Biology
- Cellular Physiology
- Human Physiology
- Genetics
- Chemistry

Business Courses:
- Marketing
- Business Law

HONORS   GPA: 3.2   Dean's List: 2 semesters

ACTIVITIES   Vice President, CSUN Biology Club
Sigma Alpha Epsilon Fraternity

**RELEVANT
EXPERIENCE
3/xx
to
present**

Customer Service Representative
BelAir Surgical Supply, Van Nuys, California
- Provide customers and 30+ outside sales personnel with product/ service information
- Open new accounts and coordinate customer relations
- Prepare sales statistics and graphs

**11/xx
to
2/xx**

Sales Associate
Sears, Roebuck and Company, Northridge, California
- Demonstrated and sold a variety of floor merchandise
- Provided customer service in high volume catalog sales department
- Supervised and trained two employees
- Opened new accounts and conducted credit checks
- Received "Employee of the Month" award

**5/xx
to
9/xx**

Manager/Trainer
Six Flags Magic Mountain, Valencia, California
- Managed three general merchandise stores
- Supervised and scheduled 40+ employees
- Trained employees to work in games and retail areas

**ADDITIONAL
EXPERIENCE**

Part-Time and Summer Employment:
Construction Worker, File Clerk, Food Service

Figure 3.5
A Sample Chronological Résumé

Even when you use the functional résumé to emphasize your skills, also include a brief chronological history of your work experience to help the employer see the continuity among jobs and the progression of responsibilities. A sample functional résumé is presented in Figure 3.6 on page 56.

The Curriculum Vitae. The **curriculum vitae** (CV; sometimes called an academic vitae) is a different kind of résumé and would be used by, for example, your college professors when applying for teaching positions or a scientist applying for a job with a pharmaceutical company. The CV is a list of your accomplishments. For example, a college professor might organize her or his CV under categories such as Education (identifying the degrees earned and the institutions from which they were earned), Publications, Courses Taught, and Service (to professional associations, to the college, and to the community). Lots of curricula vitae (CVs) are online and you may find it interesting to locate CVs of professors at your college or professors who have conducted research you've read. You can look at my CV by going to the Communication Blog (http://tcbdevito.blogspot.com) and clicking "vita." This CV is a bit more informal and selective (with asides about certain textbooks) than most academic CVs, as you'll see when you visit some of the other sites for CVs.

In addition to the suggestions offered here and on the various websites mentioned, a variety of computer programs are available to help you in preparing your résumé. Most offer an extensive array of

---

▼ ONLINE HELP

Take a look at Google Scholar (www.scholar.google.com) for information on scholars and scholarship generally. In addition to providing a useful starting place for locating curriculum vitae, it will also prove helpful in searching scholarly literature in a wide variety of fields.

templates that you fill in (or customize if you wish) with your specific data. The one presented in Figure 3.6 (page 56), for example, was customized from a Corel Office Suite template. Microsoft Word offers excellent templates; you can access the Résumé Wizard by going to File/New/New Document tab/New from Template/General Templates/Other Documents/Résumé Wizard (double click). There you'll find templates for professional, contemporary, and elegant styles and for entry-level, chronological, functional, and professional résumés.

Any résumé may be submitted in hard copy or in electronic form. The way you submit your résumé will be determined by the company to which you're applying. Often, though this is certainly changing, small organizations welcome hard copy résumés. Larger, and especially multinational, organizations may ask for electronic résumés that they can scan into a database and attempt to match their needs with the competences on the résumés. The "matchup" is done by searching for keywords, so be sure to include the terms in your résumé that you believe this employer might be looking for.

Keywords will naturally vary with the type of job in which you're interested. The best source for finding these keywords is the job description for the position you want. Note especially the nouns in the description and try to use these (when appropriate) in your résumé. Another way to find the keywords is to visit the website of the company you want to interview with as well as other companies in the same field; you'll quickly pick up the jargon of the field and some keywords you can use. And, of course, if you have the opportunity, network with people in the field; listen to how they talk and seek their expertise on keywords.

You can also post your résumé on the Internet through a variety of websites. For example, www.careermosaic.com will post your résumé for four months. At Monster.com (www.monster.com) you can post your résumé and the type of job you're looking for, and you will receive an e-mail when an appropriate job is posted (review Figure 3.3, p. 48).

① Ramona Morales
57-12 Horace Harding Expressway #15D
Corona, NY 11368
(718) 555-0005
r/morales@xyz.com

② Objective	To secure a position with a college textbook publisher in marketing and sales.
③ Employment Experience	Bookstore Assistant, Queens College Bookstore 2009–present • Maintained shelf stock • Managed inventory database • Placed orders with textbook publishers • Assisted with front desk operations, including client interaction, operating cash register, typing, and filing Front Desk Employee, Queens College Library 2007 • Responsible for periodical library • Checked books in and out at front desk • Acted as liaison for interlibrary loan books • Offered general information about college library, the online catalog system, interlibrary loans, and the Internet terminals Retail sales and management, luggage department, Macy's Department Store, Queens Center
④ Education	Queens College, BA expected 2011 Major: Communication (Emphasis on interpersonal communication and public relations) Minor: Marketing 12 Credits in Computer Science LaGuardia Community College, AA, 2002 Major: Business
⑤ Activities	• Vice President, Debate Club, Queens College, 2009–2010 • Member, Championship Debate Team, Eastern Division, 2009 • Literacy Volunteer for Spanish-speaking grade school students in English at PS 150, 2008 • Class Treasurer, LaGuardia Community College, 2006–2008 • Member, Young Business Person's Association
⑥ Skills and Competencies	• Word processing • Working knowledge of Microsoft Excel and Lotus 1-2-3 • Knowledge of HTML language inventory software • Bilingual in English and Spanish, capable in French • Excellent interpersonal and public speaking skills
⑦ References	Available upon request.
⑧	

Figure 3.6
A Sample Functional Résumé

1. Your name, address, phone and fax number, and e-mail are generally centered at the top of the résumé.

2. For some people, employment objectives may be more general than indicated here; for example, "to secure a management trainee position with an international investment bank." If you have more specific objectives, put them down. Don't imply that you'll take just anything, but don't appear too specific or demanding, either.

3. List work experience in chronological order, beginning with your latest position and working back. Depending on your work experience, you may have to pare down what you write. Or, if you have little or nothing to write, you may have to search through your employment history for some relevant experience. Often, the dates of the various positions are included. If you have little or no paid work experience or large gaps in employment history due, say, to time off raising a family, include volunteer work or other unpaid work that requires skills important to the job; for example, coordinator of a little league team or treasurer of the PTA.

4. Provide more information than simply your educational degree. For example, include your major and your minor and perhaps sequences of courses in communication or management or some other field that will further establish your suitability for the job. List honors or awards if they're relevant to your education or job experience. If the awards are primarily educational (for example, Dean's List), list them under the Education heading; if job-related, list them under the Employment Experience heading.

5. Identify those activities that are relevant to the job skills you want to demonstrate (for example, debating) as well as those that attest to the personal qualities you want to stress (for example, reliability and trustworthiness, as shown in being treasurer).

6. Highlight your special skills. Do you have some foreign language ability? Do you have experience with business or statistical software? If you do, put it down. Such competencies are relevant to many jobs.

7. Some interview experts recommend you include on your résumé the names of references, people who can attest to your abilities and character. If you do this, include these names—each with address, phone numbers, and e-mail address— at the end of the résumé under a References heading. Usually, however, you mention in your cover letter that references are available upon request.

8. Make sure your résumé creates the impression you want to make. Typographical errors, incorrect spelling, poorly spaced headings and entries, and generally sloppy work will make a negative impression.

Suggestions for Writing Your Résumé Together with the previous discussion on the types of résumés, the sample résumés, and the suggestions offered on the numerous websites, the following suggestions will help you write an effective and successful résumé.

> *Everybody looks good on paper.*
> —JOHN Y. BROWN

- Gain attention. Interviewers and recruiters spend only a few seconds looking through the pile of résumés that reach their desks. So make your résumé jump out—not with garish color or graphics but with excellence in style and format.

- Proofread, proofread, proofread. Check spelling, grammar, and punctuation as though your job depended on it, because it does.

- Use the same quality paper, laser printer, and clear and easily readable font that doesn't look like the old-fashioned typing (as Courier does) for both your résumé and your cover letter (discussed below). Laser-printed résumés scan a lot better than those written with dot matrix or bubble jet printers.

- Tell the truth. Don't make up experience, pad your GPA, or exaggerate your competences.

- Test drive your résumé. Before sending out your résumé, have others look it over and get some feedback. College career centers often offer this service; if not, then try passing it by a helpful professor or a more experienced friend.

- Include keywords in your résumé. As already noted, many résumés are scanned into huge databases and searched on the basis of keywords. Use the words that a recruiter would use in looking for someone to fulfill the job you want.

- Use powerful words. In writing your résumé, use verbs that communicate power. Here are some suggestions from résumé expert Tim Haft (1997): *management skills:* directed, formed, governed, instituted, managed, produced; *organizational skills:* coordinated, implemented, installed, planned, prepared;

communication skills: conducted, demonstrated, explained, instructed, lectured, reported; *research skills:* analyzed, audited, documented, evaluated, researched, tested; *creativity:* authored, conceived, created, designed, devised, originated.

> *A résumé is a balance sheet without any liabilities.*
>
> —ROBERT HALF

The Résumé Cover Letter Along with your résumé, send a **cover letter** and give it the same care and attention to detail that you used in creating your résumé. Here are a few suggestions:

- Follow standard format for setting up your letter. If you're unfamiliar with the format for business letters, let the word-processing wizard help you out or follow the format in the template presented in Figure 3.7 on page 60.

- Personalize your letter. Don't create one generic letter for all your applications; personalize each one for the specific job.

- Be sure to provide up-to-date and totally accurate contact information. At the same time, avoid including personal information in your letter or in your résumé. For example, your age, religion, and social security number should **not** be included.

- Don't duplicate the information in your résumé, but do express your interest in the job and your belief that you have the competences to contribute to the company.

Your mailing address
City, State Zip Code
(Area Code) Phone Number
Email address

Month Date, Year

Mr./Ms./Dr. First and Last Name of Person
Addressee's Job Title
Employer Organization's Name
Employer Street Address/P.O. Box
City, State Zip Code

Dear Mr./Ms./Dr. Last Name of Addressee:

Tell the letter recipient what position you are writing to inquire about. Indicate how you learned of the position or their organization. Give a timetable for when you will be available to start work.

Express knowledge about the duties of the position that you're writing about, as well as knowledge about the organization and its products and services. (This means you must research the potential employer.) Describe how your qualifications make you a good fit for the position. Correlate your experience (paid or voluntary) to the position or organization. Students and recent graduates may mention relevant courses and campus activities. Expand on the most relevant items included in your résumé, giving more detail about the projects and experiences that will be of particular interest to this employer.

Ask for an appointment for an interview, or tell the recipient that you will be in contact soon to discuss a mutually convenient appointment. If the employer is not close to where you live, indicate a range of days when you would be able to come for an interview. For example, if you will be in the area for a holiday break, mention those dates as an ideal time to meet. Thank the recipient for his/her time and consideration.

Sincerely,

Signature

Your name typed

Enclosure

- Keep your letter to one page; if it's too long, it might not get read.

- Express appreciation for being considered for the position and state that you look forward to a reply.

Prepare Answers and Questions

If the interview is at all important to you, you'll probably think about it for some time. Use this time productively by rehearsing (by yourself or, if possible, with friends) the predicted course of the interview.

Think about the questions that are likely to be asked and how you'll answer them. Table 3.2 presents a list of questions commonly asked in employment interviews organized around the major topics on the résumé and drawn from a variety of interviewing experts (Seidman, 1991; Kennedy, 2000; Stewart & Cash, 2008). As you read this list, visualize yourself at a job interview and try responding to the questions in the middle column. After you've formulated a specific response, look at the suggestions opposite each set of questions. Did you follow the suggestions? Can you rephrase your responses for greater effectiveness? You may also find it helpful to rehearse with this list before going into the interview. Although not all of these questions will be asked in any one interview, be prepared to answer all of them. Realize that many interviewers will base much of their impression of you on your previous performance, which they take as an indication of your future performance. Keep this in mind when you discuss your previous positions and work patterns.

◄ Figure 3.7

A Sample Résumé Cover Letter Template

The template on the previous page is one example of content and layout for a cover letter. More examples are available from the Berkeley Career Center (https://career.berkeley.edu/Guide/ResumeLetterWriting.pdf). Also take a look at St. Cloud State University's website (http://leo.stcloudstate.edu/resumes/coverlet), which includes useful information on how to write cover letters and offers a variety of sample letters. Western Michigan's career website also offers useful advice on cover letters (http://homepages.wmich.edu/~k7gunder/resumecover.htm).

TABLE 3.2 **Common Interview Questions**

As you read through this table, consider how you'd answer these common questions.

Question Areas	Possible Questions	Suggested Responses
Objectives and Career Goals	What made you apply to Datacomm? Do you know much about Datacomm? What do you like most about Datacomm? If you took a job with us, where would you like to be in five years? What benefits do you want to get out of this job?	Be positive (and as specific as you can be) about the company. Demonstrate your knowledge of the company. Take a long-range view; no firm wants to hire someone who will be looking for another job in six months.
Education	What do you think of the education you got at Queens College? Why did you major in communication? What was majoring in communication at Queens like? What kinds of courses did you take? Did you do an internship? What were your responsibilities? Were computer skills integrated into the courses?	Be positive about your educational experience. Try to relate your educational experience to the specific job. Demonstrate competence but at the same time the willingness to continue your education (either formally or informally).
Previous Work Experience	Tell me about your previous work experience. What did you do exactly? Did you enjoy working at Happy Publications? Why did you leave? How does this previous experience relate to the work you'd be doing here at Datacomm? What kinds of problems did you encounter at your last position?	Again, be positive; never knock a previous job or employer. If you do, the interviewer will think you may be criticizing them in the near future. Especially avoid bad-mouthing specific people with whom you worked.

Question Areas	Possible Questions	Suggested Responses
Special Competences	I see here you have a speaking and writing knowledge of Spanish. Could you talk with someone on the phone in Spanish or write letters in Spanish to our customers? Do you know any other languages? How much do you know about computers? Do you know Excel? PowerPoint? Accessing databases? Could you prepare company brochures and newsletters?	Before going into the interview, review your competences. Explain your skills in as much detail as needed to establish their relevance to the job and your own specific competences.
Personal	Tell me who you are. What do you like? What do you dislike? Are you willing to relocate? Are there places you would not consider relocating to? Do you think you'd have any trouble giving orders to others? Do you have difficulty working under deadlines?	Place yourself in the position of the interviewer and ask yourself what kind of person you would hire. Stress your ability to work independently but also as a member of a team. Stress your flexibility in adapting to new work situations.
References	Do the people you listed here know you personally or academically? Which of these people know you the best? Who would give you the best reference? Who else might know about your abilities that we might contact that isn't listed here?	Be sure the people you list know you well and especially that they have special knowledge about you that is relevant to the job at hand.

(Continued)

TABLE 3.2 **Common Interview Questions** *(Continued)*

Question Areas	Possible Questions	Suggested Responses
Questions You Want to Ask the Interviewer	What would you like to ask me? Are there things about XYZ you would like to know?	Don't say you have no questions. Ask something about issues not fully covered in the interview. And surely there are aspects of the company that you would like to know about. Ask, but do so positively and politely.

Also consider preparing some explanation for anything that the interviewer might have learned about you from your messages and photos on social networking sites that might at first glance appear less than flattering. In one study, approximately half of the college students surveyed expected their potential employer to view their website profile (2008 Graduating Student Survey, National Association of Colleges and Employers, www.naceweb/org, accessed 9/13/2008). The practice of employers seeking out information that is not in the standard résumé is surely increasing and the digital age has made it very easy.

Even though the interviewer will ask most of the questions, you too will want to ask questions. In addition to rehearsing some

---

▼ ONLINE HELP

The career website of the University of North Carolina at Chapel Hill has a detailed section on résumés, identifying the kinds of information you should include and showing sample chronological résumés (www.unc .edu/depts/career). Cal State at San Bernardino also maintains an excellent website with sample chronological, functional, and combination résumés (http://career.csusb.edu).

The Best and the Worst

Here are some common employment interview questions. For each question, formulate what you think would be the best possible answer (an answer that will increase your chances of getting the job) and the worst possible answer (an answer that is likely to hurt your chances of getting the job). As you develop your responses, keep in mind what employers are looking for. According to *Monster Careers: Interviewing* (Taylor, 2005) this includes: (1) relevant skills (Do you have the skills required for the job?); (2) predicted productivity over time (Will you be an asset to the company over the next however many years?); (3) understanding of the job (Do you know about the job you're applying for? Do you know how to handle such a position effectively?); (4) interaction and communication skills (Are you competent in a wide variety of interactions?); and (5) growth potential (Will you be able to grow with the company?).

Discussing your answers in small groups or with people more experienced in interviewing will help you polish your employment interviewing skills.

1. How did you like working at your last job, at ABCD?
2. What were your responsibilities at ABCD?
3. Why did you apply for this particular position here at XYZ?
4. What did you think of the preparation for this job that you received at Queens College?
5. How do you feel about traveling as a part of your job?
6. What do you do in your spare time?
7. Why do you feel qualified for this particular position?
8. What are your expectations for this job?
9. Do you prefer to work alone or as part of a team?
10. What would you like to ask me?
11. What are your greatest strengths? Your greatest weaknesses?
12. What would your ideal job look like?
13. How do you view yourself? More as an information person or more as a people person?

answers to predicted questions, fix firmly in mind the questions you want to ask the interviewer. If this were an interview for a college teaching position, you might ask about the opportunities to develop new courses or for team teaching, the facilities for computerizing instruction, or the interests of the students at the college.

After the preparations, you're ready for the actual interview. Several suggestions may guide you through this sometimes difficult procedure.

Present Yourself Effectively

This is probably the most important part of the entire procedure. If you fail here and make a bad initial impression, it will be difficult to salvage the rest of the interview, so devote special care to the way you present yourself.

> *It isn't fair, it isn't scientific, it isn't even smart, but it's a fact of life: a good first impression opens an interviewer's mind; a bad first impression closes it.*
> —JEFF TAYLOR

Bring with you the appropriate materials, whatever they may be. At the very least bring a pen and paper, an extra copy or two of your résumé, and, if appropriate, a business card. If you're applying for a job in an area in which you've worked before, you might bring samples of your previous work. If you have the opportunity, ask what materials you should bring.

An interesting perspective on self-presentation is provided by the theory of self-monitoring, which argues that you regulate (often automatically and without any conscious thought) the way you present yourself to best achieve the effect you want (Snyder, 1987). So if you think the interviewer favors an outspoken and direct style, you'll present yourself as outspoken and direct. Self-monitoring, as you can appreciate, is especially prevalent in the employment interview, where so much depends on your making the right impression.

If you're interviewing at even a reasonably successful organization, then you're likely to be facing an interviewer who is sophisticated and who will be able to pick up on your subtle cues that may indicate annoyance, lack of confidence, lack of adequate preparation, or any other feeling that might be evaluated negatively. If you're a beginning job seeker, you're not likely to fool a seasoned interviewer. And this realization should actually

> *When they ask about hobbies, you must tell them the only hobbies you enjoy are active ones. . . . You participate in sports, particularly status sports such as golf or tennis. You're not an observer, you're an active participant.*
> —JOHN T. MOLLOY

provide a comforting thought: Because the interviewer, you assume, is going to see the real you, you might as well be yourself (but yourself at your best). In "being yourself" you'll feel more comfortable and will be likely to communicate more effectively and present yourself with greater confidence.

Another part of self presentation is to shake hands appropriately. Even if you assume you know how to shake hands, take a look at Table 3.3 on page 68. As you can imagine, cultural differences may create intercultural difficulties and misunderstandings in many interpersonal situations. For example, if you shake hands in a culture that hugs and kisses, you may appear standoffish and unwilling to be close. And if you hug and kiss in a culture that is used to shaking hands, you may seem presumptuous and overly friendly. In the interview situation in the United States and in much of the world, the handshake is the appropriate form of greeting. In many Asian cultures, a bow would take the place of the handshake.

Dress for Interview Success

Many jobs are won or lost on the basis of physical appearance alone, so also give attention to your physical presentation. Unfortunately, there is no universally appropriate attire for an interview. It depends on a number of factors, perhaps first of which is the job itself. Generally, low-level jobs (cashiers in fast-food restaurants, for example) have fewer dress requirements than higher-level jobs. In fact, the

TABLE 3.3 **The Essential Handshake**

A few dos and don'ts for shaking hands in the United States:

Do	Don't
1. Make eye contact at the beginning and maintain it throughout the handshake.	Look away from the person or down at the floor or at your shaking hand.
2. Smile and otherwise signal positiveness.	Appear static or negative.
3. Extend your entire right hand.	Extend just your fingers or your left hand.
4. Grasp the other person's hand firmly.	Use so much pressure that it would be uncomfortable or grasp the other person's fingers as if you really don't want to shake hands but you're making a gesture to be polite.
5. Pump three times. A handshake in the United States lasts about 3 to 4 seconds. In other cultures, it might be shorter; more often, it's longer.	Give the person a "dead fish" or pump much more than three times.
6. Release your grasp while still maintaining eye contact.	Hold your grasp for an overly long time or release it too early.

higher you go up the hierarchy, the more formal, more conservative, and more expensive your clothing should be. Even this seemingly simple advice has to be qualified; some high-level tech companies are probably more relaxed about clothing than are firms offering lower-level jobs in traditionally conservative fields such as law.

If you want to succeed, you'd better look as if you mean business.

—JEANNE HOLM

Nevertheless, here are a few general dress suggestions. First, discover what the accepted and appropriate attire for the company is by visiting the company and taking careful note of the way the people dress. Then dress one or two levels more conservatively or, as one interview guide puts it, "Dress as well as the best person you see" (Taylor, 2005). The interviewer is likely to expect this.

Second, avoid excess in just about anything you can think of. Too much jewelry, cologne, or any one particular color is likely to call attention to your manner of dress instead of to who you are and what your competencies are.

Third, dress comfortably but not too casually. Comfortable clothing will make you feel more at ease and will help you to be yourself. If you're in doubt as to how casually you should dress, err on the side of formality; wear the tie, high heels, or dress.

Fourth, consider any outward display of body piercings and facial and hand tattoos. Although people wearing such body jewelry, for example, may wish to communicate positive meanings, those interpreting these messages seem to infer that the wearer is communicating an unwillingness to conform to social norms and a willingness to take greater risks than those without such adornments (Forbes, 2001)—qualities that may work against your "fitting in." It's also worth noting that in a study of employers' perceptions, applicants with eyebrow piercings were rated and ranked significantly lower than those without such piercings (Acor, 2001).

Tattoos—temporary or permanent—may be popular at the clubs but may work against you in a job interview. Tattooed students see themselves as more adventurous, creative, individualistic, and

---

▼ ONLINE HELP

A good guide to dressing to impress is Washington State University's website (http://amdt.wsu.edu/research/dti/). But, online catalogs (try those of the stores that you suspect the people at the company would shop at) are also excellent guides to how to dress for the interview.

risk-taking than those without tattoos (Drews, Allison, & Probst, 2000). Whether employers will see the same qualities, however, is another issue.

Arrive on Time

In interview situations, "on time" means 5 to 10 minutes early. This brief period will allow you time to relax, to get accustomed to the general surroundings, and perhaps to fill out any forms that may be required. And it gives you a cushion should something delay you on the way.

Make sure you know the name of the company, the job title, and the interviewer's name. Although you'll have much on your mind when you go into the interview, the interviewer's name is not one of the things you can afford to forget (or mispronounce).

In presenting yourself, don't err on the side of too much casualness or too much formality. When there's doubt, act on the side of increased formality. Slouching back in the chair, smoking, and chewing gum or candy are obvious behaviors to avoid when you're trying to impress an interviewer.

Demonstrate Effective Interpersonal Communication

Earlier the characteristics of effective interpersonal communication were identified. You may find it helpful at this point to review them (pp. 19–22). Try your best to demonstrate these characteristics throughout the interview.

Acknowledge Cultural Rules and Customs

Each culture—and each organization is much like a culture—has its own rules for communicating (Barna, 1991; Ruben, 1985; Spitzberg, 1991; Spitzberg & Cupach, 2002). These **cultural rules**—whether in the interview situation or in friendly conversation—prescribe appropriate and inappropriate behavior, rewards and punishments, and what will help you get the job and what won't. For example, general

Displaying Communication Confidence in the Employment Interview

Presented below is a brief dialogue that might take place during an initial interview for a job. Read through the transcript and identify the elements that demonstrate the possession of or the lack of confidence and indicate how the applicant might have better represented herself as a more confident, more in-control type of individual. How you would have demonstrated confidence in responding to each of Ms. Bass's questions? *What specific signals are the most important in communicating confidence in an interview?*

Ms. Bass: And you are?

Linda: Sir? I mean Mrs., madam. Me? Er, I mean, yeah. Yeah, I'm Linda. Miss Giddeon. Linda Giddeon.

Ms. Bass: So, Ms. Giddeon, what can I do for you?

Linda: I'm here for, I mean I'm applying for that job, right?

Ms. Bass: So, you'd like a job with Datacomm. Is that right?

Linda: Well, er, yes. I guess so. I think I'd like that.

Ms. Bass: Tell me what you know about computers.

Linda: Well, I didn't take that many courses. But, I took some. Some good ones. Some were too time-consuming, so I didn't take them.

Ms. Bass: Well, tell me what you did take.

Linda: Well, I guess, I mean I took the regular courses. Here's my transcript.

Ms. Bass: I can read your transcript. But, I want to hear from you, exactly what you know about computers.

Linda: Well, I took courses in different aspects of computers. Programming I and II. And I took desktop publishing. Courses like that.

(Continued)

Ms. Bass: Instead of telling me your courses, tell me what you know.

Linda: Excuse me. I guess I'm a little nervous. I'm not very good at interviewing. In fact, this is my first interview and I really don't know what to say.

Ms. Bass: (Smiling) Are you sure you were a computer major?

Linda: Yes.

Ms. Bass: Okay, I know. Let me put it this way: Do you think you can do anything for Datacomm?

Linda: Oh. Yes. I mean, I may be wrong about this but I'm pretty sure, I could do a lot, really a lot for Datacomm.

Ms. Bass: OK, Ms. Giddeon, now exactly what can you do for Datacomm that the next applicant can't do better?

Linda: Oh, well, I really don't know much about Datacomm. I mean, I may be wrong about this, but I thought I would assist someone and learn the job that way.

Ms. Bass: Right. What skills can you bring to Datacomm? Why would you make such a good learner?

Linda: Gee, this isn't as easy as I thought it would be.

Ms. Bass: Ms. Giddeon, tell me what you are especially good at.

Linda: Well, I guess I'm kind of good at getting along with people—you know, working with people in groups.

Ms. Bass: No, I'm not sure I know what that means. Tell me.

Linda: Like, I mean I'm pretty good at just working with people. People think I'm kind of neat. You know, like, people like me. I don't know, I guess it's just my personality.

Ms. Bass: I don't doubt that, Ms. Giddeon, but do you have any other talents—other than being "neat"?

Linda: I can run a desktop publishing program. Is that important?

Ms. Bass: Ms. Giddeon, everything is important.

Linda: Is there anything else?

Ms. Bass: I don't know, Ms. Giddeon, is there anything else?

Linda: I don't know.

Ms. Bass: I want to thank you for your time, Ms. Giddeon. We'll be in touch with you.

Linda: Oh, I got the job?

Ms. Bass: Not exactly. If we decide on you, we will call you.

Linda: Like, I mean, you can't tell me now?

Ms. Bass: No, sorry.

Linda: That's cool.

advice was given earlier to emphasize your positive qualities, to highlight your abilities, and to minimize any negative characteristics or failings. But in some cultures—especially collectivist cultures such as China, Korea, and Japan—interviewees are expected to show modesty (Copeland & Griggs, 1985). Should you stress your own competences too much, you may be seen as arrogant, brash, and unfit to work in an organization in which teamwork and cooperation are valued and expected.

In collectivist cultures, great deference is to be shown to the interviewer, who represents the company. If you don't treat the interviewer with great respect, you may appear to be disrespectful of the entire company. On the other hand, in an individualist culture such as the United States, too much deference may make you appear unassertive, unsure of yourself, and unable to assume a position of authority.

And recall (as mentioned earlier) that cultures also vary greatly in attitudes toward directness. Too direct an approach may offend people of one culture, whereas too indirect an approach might offend people of another.

If you are going to a job interview for a company with a strong international presence and you suspect you may be interviewed by a person from a culture very different from your own, take a look at some of the excellent books on this subject. Books by Noreen Dresser (1999, 2005) and Roger Axtell (1990, 1993, 2007) are excellent starting places, as are many websites. Search for "intercultural and business" and similar terms.

Mentally Review the Interview

By reviewing the interview, you'll fix it firmly in your mind. What questions were asked? How did you answer them? Review and write down any important information the interviewer gave. Ask yourself what you could have done more effectively. Consider what you did effectively that you could repeat in other interviews. Ask yourself how you might correct your weaknesses and capitalize on your strengths.

Follow Up

Follow up an interview with a letter. All **follow-up letters** should include an expression of thanks for the interview, however, the letter can serve any number of additional purposes. Among the most important of these are:

> *A candidate who follows up with interviewers can overcome competition with more experience, more skills, or a smoother interview style. The reason is simple: follow-up continues the relationship.*
>
> —JEFF TAYLOR

- to recall the interview, to stress your continued interest in the position, and to reiterate one or two of your greatest assets for this job

- to add information not covered in the interview or that happened after the interview

- to inquire about the position if you haven't received a response by a preset or some reasonable amount of time

- to keep the door open after rejection for the possibility of a similar opening in the near future

Writing the Follow-Up Letter

Select one of the following situations and write a brief follow-up letter. Use fictional names for yourself and the interviewer.

- Letter to thank the interviewee for the information interview
- Letter to thank the interviewer for the job interview
- Letter to request information because you haven't had any response about the job
- Letter to express regret at not getting the job

You may find it helpful to form groups of five or six and discuss these letters in terms of their effectiveness to achieve your purpose. You may also want to get some feedback from experts in the field.

Figures 3.8, 3.9, and 3.10 provide examples of follow-up letters that include these functions; the notes on facing pages identify, more specifically, the various goals.

The Lawfulness of Questions

Through the Equal Employment Opportunity Commission, the federal government has classified some interview questions as unlawful. These are federal guidelines and therefore apply in all 50 states; individual states, however, may have additional restrictions. You may find it interesting to take the following self-test (constructed with the good help of Stewart & Cash, 2008; Zincoff & Goyer, 1984; Kirby, 2001) to see if you can identify which questions are lawful and which are unlawful (see Pullum, 1991).

> 'Tis not every question that deserves an answer.
> —THOMAS FULLER

123 Main Street
Accord, New York 12404
(845) 555-1234
Rita.Williams@nomail.com

Ms. Claire Trevor
ABC Books
321 Elm Street
Kingston, New York 12426

December 1, 2010

Dear Ms. Trevor:

1 Thank you for interviewing me on November 30, 2010 for the position of editorial
assistant. As I mentioned at the interview, I'm very interested in the position; it's
exactly what I'm looking for.

2 As we discussed during the interview, I've had an extensive background in
English and communication—the areas you noted as crucial to the position.
And, although we didn't have time to discuss it, I'm also competent in all
the Microsoft Office programs for both PC and Mac.

3 I also want to add that just yesterday I was appointed editor of the college
newspaper, a position I'll hold until graduation in June. It's going to be an
exciting adventure; I'm looking forward to the challenge.

4 Again, thank you for your consideration. I look forward to hearing from you.

Sincerely,

Rita Williams

Rita Williams

Figure 3.8
**A Sample Follow-Up Letter to Reiterate Interest and Competences
and to Add New Information**

1 This paragraph thanks the interviewer, recalls the interview, and reiterates your interest in the position. Avoid going into too much detail; the letter should not be longer than one page.

2 Here you restate your major assets or competencies and even add one that wasn't discusssed at the interview. Avoid overdoing this. Your résumé and your interview should have accomplished this general goal of establishing your competencies. Use this letter as a brief reminder.

3 This adds new information and, in this case, demonstrates your confidence, willingness to take on major responsibilities, and a recognition by others of your competence to handle such a position.

4 A simple closing of thanks and continued interest will serve well here.

123 Main Street
Accord, New York 12404
(845) 555-1234
Rita.Williams@nomail.com

Ms. Claire Trevor
ABC Books
321 Elm Street
Kingston, New York 12426

December 1, 2010

Dear Ms. Trevor:

① I'm very sorry to hear that I was not selected for the position of editorial assistant for which I interviewed on November 30, 2010.

② I'm still very interested in working at ABC Books and hope that you'll consider me for any similar positions that may open in the near future.

③ I'm continuing my preparation to enter publishing by taking Advanced Editing and Print Media this semester and a course in Publishing Economics at the Learning Annex.

④ If you have a moment, I'd much appreciate any feedback you might want to give me to help me in future interviews. I'm especially concerned with learning how I can strengthen both my résumé and my interviewing for similar positions.

⑤ Thank you for your time and consideration.

Sincerely,

Rita Williams

Rita Williams

Figure 3.9
A Sample Follow-Up Letter to Keep the Doors Open after Rejection

1 Here you recall the interview and state your disappointment in not being hired. Avoid blaming ("I didn't feel well that day" or "I was nervous") or guessing why you didn't get the job ("I guess my grades weren't that good").

2 Here you reiterate your interest in the company and ask that you continue to be considered for another, similar position. Any more than this would be too much.

3 Here you add to your list of assets that may make your résumé look better than it did originally. It demonstrates your commitment to the field and your focus on improving your knowledge and skills.

4 If you're beginning your employment interviewing, it's often helpful to get professional feedback on your résumé as well as on your interviewing technique. Many interviewers will be reluctant to be as honest as you'd like them to be but some may say something you'll find useful in subsequent interviews. At times, this request for feedback is communicated in a separate letter. This paragraph provides an example of what you might say.

5 A simple expression of appreciation will work best as a closing.

123 Main Street
Accord, New York 12404
(845) 555-1234
Rita.Williams@nomail.com

Ms. Claire Trevor
ABC Books
321 Elm Street
Kingston, New York 12426

December 7, 2010

Dear Ms. Trevor:

1 I interviewed for the position of editorial assistant on October 5, 2010, and I'm wondering if you've made a decision. My résumé and other application materials are on file at your office. If there is any additional information I can supply, please let me know.

2 I am very interested in working at ABC Books and feel that my academic courses, my work on the student newspaper, and my lifelong love of books would make me a great editorial assistant.

3 Thank you for your time and consideration. I look forward to hearing from you.

Sincerely,

Rita Williams

Rita Williams

Figure 3.10
Sample Follow-Up Letter to Inquire Whether a Decision Has Been Made

1 At times, it may be necessary to inquire as to whether a decision has been made. For example, if this job is your first choice but your second choice made you an offer, then it's important to make inquiry. But it's probably not a good idea to say, for example, that you've received another offer that you'll take if you don't get a reply soon. Always inquire courteously (even if your natural inclination is to be annoyed at the delay); there may be quite reasonable explanations for the delay. Even if there aren't, it won't help your case to blame your employer of choice. Asking if you can send any additional information you can helps to stress your continued interest in the position.

2 Here you reiterate your interest in the company and your major assets—briefly but clearly.

3 A simple thank you and a reasonable request to hear some kind of response.

CAN YOU IDENTIFY UNLAWFUL QUESTIONS?

For each question write L (lawful) if you think the question is legal for an interviewer to ask in an employment interview and U (unlawful) if you think the question is illegal. For each question you consider unlawful, indicate why you think it's so classified.

_____ ❶ Are you married, Tom?

_____ ❷ When did you graduate from high school, Mary?

_____ ❸ Do you have a picture so I can attach it to your résumé?

_____ ❹ Will you need to be near a mosque (church, synagogue)?

_____ ❺ I see you took a course in "gay and lesbian studies." Are you gay?

_____ ❻ Is Chinese your native language?

_____ ❼ Will you have difficulty getting a babysitter?

_____ ❽ I notice that you walk with a limp. Is this a permanent injury?

_____ ❾ Where were you born?

_____ ❿ Have you ever been arrested for a crime?

_____ ⑪ How tall are you? How much do you weigh?

_____ ⑫ I see you were in the Army. Were you honorably discharged?

All twelve questions are unlawful. The remaining discussion illustrates why each of these and similar questions are unlawful.

Recognizing Unlawful Questions   Some of the more important areas in which **unlawful questions** are frequently asked concern age, marital status, race, religion, nationality, citizenship, physical condition, and arrest and criminal records. For example, it's legal to ask applicants whether they meet the legal age requirements for the job and could provide proof of that. But it's unlawful to ask their exact age, even in indirect ways, as illustrated in question 2 in the self-test. It's unlawful to ask about a person's marital status (question 1) or about family matters that are unrelated to the job (question 7). An interviewer may ask you, however, to identify a close relative or guardian if you're a minor or any relative who currently works for the company.

Questions concerning your race (questions 3 and 6), religion (question 4), national origin (question 9), affectional orientation (question 5), age (question 2), handicaps unrelated to job performance (question 8), or even arrest record (question 10) are unlawful, as are questions that get at this same information in oblique ways. For example, requiring a picture may be a way of discriminating against an applicant on the basis of sex, race, or age.

Thus, for example, the interviewer may ask you what languages you're fluent in but may not ask what your native language is (question 6), what language you speak at home, or what language your parents speak. The interviewer may ask you if you are in this country legally but may not ask if you were born in this country or naturalized (question 9). The interviewer may ask about the type of training you received in the military but not if you were honorably discharged (question 12).

The interviewer may inquire into your physical condition only insofar as the job is concerned. For example, the interviewer may ask, "Do you have any physical problems that might prevent you from fulfilling the responsibilities of this job?" But the interviewer may not ask about any physical disabilities (question 8) or about your height or weight (question 11). The interviewer may ask you if

---

▼ ONLINE HELP

If you have questions about disability disclosure and interviewing, take a look at Jan's Consultants' Corner (www.jan.wvu.edu/corner/vol01/iss13.htm).

you've been convicted of a felony but not if you've been arrested (question 10).

These are merely examples of some of the lawful and unlawful questions that may be asked during an interview. Note that even the questions used as examples here might be lawful in specific situations. The test to apply is simple: Is the information requested related to your ability to perform the job? Such questions are referred to as **BFOQ—bona fide occupational qualification**—questions.

> *The things most people want to know are usually none of their business.*
> —GEORGE BERNARD SHAW

Once you've discovered what kinds of questions are unlawful, consider how to deal with them if they come up during an interview.

Dealing with Unlawful Questions There are three main approaches to dealing with unlawful questions. In selecting your approach, realize that answering or not answering a question—whether it is legal or illegal—may well make the difference between getting the job and not getting the job. Keep this in mind as you select your strategy. Also, note that at times an interviewer may ask a question that is technically illegal but may not even know it's illegal. Or the interviewer may have no discriminatory or negative motives for asking it.

Answer the Question. The most obvious strategy is to simply answer the question, assuming you have no reason to suspect any negative motives on the part of the interviewer and you don't mind answering this question, even though you know it's illegal. And do realize that even when a question is technically illegal, your not answering it may work against your getting the job. The interviewer

▼ **ONLINE HELP**

The career services department of Minot State University maintains a useful website on interviewing techniques and sample questions (www .minotstateu.edu/careers/interviewingtechniques.html).

may see you as unnecessarily argumentative and not a cooperative future member of the team.

Answer the Question (In Part). Another strategy is to answer the part of the question you don't object to and omit any information you don't want to give. For example, if you're asked an unlawful question concerning what language is spoken at home, you may respond with a statement such as "I have some language facility in German and Italian," without specifying a direct answer to the question. If you're asked to list all the organizations of which you're a member (an unlawful question in many states, because it's often a way of getting at political affiliation, religion, nationality, and various other areas), you might respond by saying something like: "The only organizations I belong to that are relevant to this job are the International Communication Association and the National Communication Association."

This type of response is preferable to the one that immediately tells the interviewer she or he is asking an unlawful question, which can easily create an adversarial relationship pitting you against the interviewer. As already noted, it's possible that the interviewer isn't even aware of the legality of various questions and may have no intention of trying to get at information you're not obliged to give. For example, the interviewer may recognize the nationality of your last name and simply want to mention that she or he is also of that nationality. If you immediately take issue with the question, you may be creating problems where none really exist.

INTERVIEWING CHOICE POINT At a job interview, the interviewer continually returns to your age. You are a bit old for the job, but you know you can be successful and you really want the job. You also know that this is an illegal question. *What options do you have for dealing with this question but not alienating the interviewer? What might you say?*

On the other hand, recognize that in many employment interviews the unwritten intention is to keep certain people out, whether it's people who are older or those of a particular marital status, affectional orientation, nationality, religion, and so on. If you're confronted by questions that are unlawful and that you don't want to answer, and if the gentle methods described above don't work and your interviewer persists—saying, for example, "Is German the language spoken at home?" or "What other organizations have you belonged to?"—you might counter by saying that such information is irrelevant to the interview and to the position you're seeking. Again, be courteous but firm. Say something like, "This position does not call for any particular language skill and so it does not matter what language is spoken in my home." Or you might say, "The organizations I mentioned are the only relevant ones; whatever other organizations I belong to will certainly not interfere with my ability to perform in this company at this job."

INTERVIEWING EXERCISE

Responding to Unlawful Questions

This exercise is designed to raise some of the unlawful questions that you don't have to answer and provide you with practice in developing responses that protect your privacy while maintaining a positive relationship with the interviewer. In the self-test, Can You Identify Unlawful Questions? 12 questions were presented. Assuming that you do not want to answer the questions, how would you respond to each of them? One useful procedure is to write your responses and then compare them with those of other students, either in groups or with the class as a whole. Or form two-person groups and role-play the interviewer–interviewee situation. To make this exercise realistic, the person playing the interviewer should press for an answer, while the interviewee should continue to avoid answering, yet respond positively and cordially. You'll discover this is not always easy; tempers often flare in this type of interaction.

Explain Your Reasons for Not Answering. If the interviewer still persists—and it's doubtful that many would after these rather clear and direct responses—you might note that these questions are unlawful and that you'd rather not answer them. This response at least gives you a convenient way out of the situation just in case the interviewer didn't realize that these questions are, in fact, illegal. Again, if the interviewer persists and you don't want to answer the questions, say so.

A worksheet to help you prepare for your employment interview follows.

EMPLOYMENT INTERVIEW PREPARATION GUIDE

Before entering the employment interview, prepare yourself by completing the following questionnaire. It will not be easy; in fact, it's likely to prove frustrating and quite difficult. But it will be helpful. This preparation will make you more informed and more focused, help you anticipate and practice likely interview questions and answers, and put you more at ease and in control of the interview process.

This preparation guide may appear much like an extended cheat sheet (pp. 9–10). It is exactly that. The best approach is to prepare the detailed guide presented here and then reduce it to its essentials for your cheat sheet.

1. **Information about yourself.** What do you want the interviewer to know and notice about you? In the left column, list four things about yourself that are not on your résumé that you want to highlight, and in the right column, indicate how you'll communicate these things to the interviewer.

Things about Myself That I Want the Interviewer to Know	How I'll Communicate These Things to the Interviewer
1. _____	1. _____
2. _____	2. _____

3. _____

   _____

   _____

   _____

   _____

4. _____

   _____

   _____

   _____

3. _____

   _____

   _____

   _____

   _____

4. _____

   _____

   _____

   _____

2. **Knowledge of company.** Will you be able to demonstrate your knowledge of the company (for example, its primary and secondary businesses, its immediate and long-term objectives, its competition)? Write a paragraph demonstrating your knowledge about the company that includes at least three facts that might prove relevant during the interview.

_____
_____
_____
_____
_____
_____
_____
_____
_____
_____
_____

3. **Knowledge of position.** Will you be able to demonstrate your knowledge of the position for which you're applying (the qualifications, the responsibilities, how this job fits in with the entire organization, salary range)? Write a paragraph that includes at least three facts about the position that might prove relevant during the interview.

4. **Special skills.** What special skills or competences might you be asked about (for example, what presentation skills do you have?) and how might you demonstrate your competences (for example, you took a class in public speaking and used Power-Point throughout the course)?

Special Skills I Might Be Asked About

1. _____

_____

_____

_____

2. _____

_____

_____

How I'll Demonstrate These Skills

1. _____

_____

_____

_____

2. _____

_____

_____

3. _____   3. _____
   _____   _____
   _____   _____
   _____   _____
   _____   _____
   _____   _____
   _____   _____
4. _____   4. _____
   _____   _____
   _____   _____
   _____   _____
   _____   _____

5. **Information to learn.** What do you want to learn from the
   interviewer? List four things you want to find out about during
   the interview (about the job, about the company, about your
   potential role in the company, about salary, etc.) and how you
   might discover these during the interview.

Information I Want to Know	How I'll Discover This Information
1. _____	1. _____
_____	_____
_____	_____
_____	_____
_____	_____
2. _____	2. _____
_____	_____

3. _____   3. _____

_____   _____

_____   _____

_____   _____

_____   _____

_____   _____

4. _____   4. _____

_____   _____

_____   _____

_____   _____

_____   _____

6. **Contributions.** What can you contribute to the company? List four things you can do for the company that you may want to bring out during the interview. Next to each one, indicate what you can say to demonstrate your ability to make these contributions.

Contributions I Can Make

Evidence That I Can Make Such Contributions

1. _____   1. _____

_____   _____

_____   _____

_____   _____

_____   _____

2. _____   2. _____

_____   _____

3. _____ 3. _____

4. _____ 4. _____

7. **Likely questions.** What are you likely to be asked? List four
   questions that you'll possibly be asked and what you believe to
   be effective answers. If you anticipate problems (for example, on
   the basis of experience, education, age, or any number of other
   issues), include the questions that might raise these issues along
   with your anticipated answers.

Possible Questions   **Possible Answers I Could Give**
I May Be Asked

1. _____ 1. _____

2. _____   2. _____
   _____   _____
   _____   _____
   _____   _____
   _____   _____
3. _____   3. _____
   _____   _____
   _____   _____
   _____   _____
   _____   _____
4. _____   4. _____
   _____   _____
   _____   _____
   _____   _____
   _____   _____

8. **Unlawful questions.** What unlawful questions might you be asked? List three unlawful questions you may be asked and the way in which you could answer them.

Possible Unlawful Questions I May Be Asked   **Possible Answers I Could Give**

1. _____   1. _____
   _____   _____
   _____   _____
   _____   _____
   _____   _____

2. _____

3. _____

2. _____

3. _____

Summary of Concepts and Skills

This book introduced the process of interviewing, explored the nature of questions and answers, and identified the major forms of interviewing (focusing on information-gathering and employment interviews).

1. Interviewing is a form of interpersonal communication in which two persons interact, largely through a question-and-answer format, to achieve specific goals.

2. The interview process can, for convenience, be visualized as a series of stages: opening, feedforward, questions and answers, feedback, and closing.

3. Among the types of interview structures are the informal interview, the guided interview, the standard open interview, and the quantitative interview.

4. Interviews may take place through varied channels—face-to-face, phone, and online—and may be individual or group.

5. Questions may be viewed as varying in their degree of bias (whether neutral or leading), openness, primacy (whether primary or follow-up), and directness.

6. Among the skills of interpersonal communication that are crucial to the successful interview are openness, positiveness, immediacy, interaction management, expressiveness, other-orientation, cultural sensitivity, flexibility, and confidence.

7. Like all communication, interviewing involves questions of ethics, of right and wrong.

8. In information interviews, follow these guidelines: select the person you wish to interview, secure an appointment, prepare your ques-

tions, establish rapport with the interviewee, ask permission to tape the interview, ask open-ended questions, and close and follow up the interview.

9. Especially important to the job interview is the résumé, which may be chronological, functional, or in the form of a curriculum vitae, and the cover letter that accompanies the résumé.

10. In employment interviews, follow these guidelines: prepare yourself intellectually and physically for the interview, establish your objectives, prepare answers to predicted questions, present yourself effectively, mentally review the interview, and close and follow up the interview.

11. Familiarize yourself with possible unlawful questions and develop strategies for dealing with them in a job interview.

Throughout, this book stressed the practical skills of interviewing. Place a check mark next to those skills you feel you need to work on.

_____ 1. I follow the basic guidelines in conducting information interviews.

_____ 2. Before the interview, I prepare myself intellectually and physically, establish my objectives as clearly as I can, and prepare answers to predicted questions.

_____ 3. During the interview, I present myself effectively and demonstrate effective interpersonal communication skills.

_____ 4. After the interview, I mentally review the interview and follow it up with a letter.

_____ 5. I can frame and respond appropriately to questions varying in terms of neutral–leading, open–closed, primary–follow-up, and direct–indirect.

_____ 6. I can recognize and respond appropriately to unlawful questions.

Postscript

Continuing Your Study of **Interviewing**

Interviewing is likely to be a significant part of your professional life throughout your career, so it would help if you renewed your skills periodically and kept abreast of the latest thinking about effective interviewing. There are lots of ways to do this.

When you're in a bookstore—a brick-and-mortar or an online one—take a look at the interviewing section. If something seems particularly interesting or relevant, read it. Here, for example, are some useful textbooks designed for a full-semester's course in interviewing: *Interviewing: Principles and Practices* (Stewart & Cash, 2008); *Interviewing: Speaking, Listening, and Learning for Professional Life* (Anderson & Killenberg, 2008); and *Interviewing: Situations and Contexts* (Powell & Amsbary, 2006). Any one of these would make a suitable follow-up and extension of what is presented here.

Most web browsers frequently highlight articles on interviewing. Make it a practice to look at these occasionally. If you want more articles, set a Google alert to "interviewing tips" or, if you really want lots of references, use "interviewing" without modification. When you see something that might prove interesting, take a look at it or save it to an "interviewing" folder. The websites cited throughout this book will keep you busy for quite some time and will help you master the skills of this most important form of communication.

If you want more experience in interviewing, take a course (or another course) in interviewing, either in college or at your local adult education center.

You can also learn a great deal about interviewing—what you should do and what you shouldn't do—from television news, business programs, and the familiar talk shows—everything from Jerry

Springer, Maury Povich, Jay Leno, Ellen Degeneres, Oprah Winfrey, and David Letterman to Barbara Walters, Katie Couric, Charlie Rose, and Bill Moyers. Make it a practice to view these on occasion, focusing on the techniques of interviewing each uses.

Newspapers and magazines often publish interviews with noted figures. These are often models of brevity; as you'll see, most such interviews cover just the kinds of things you'd want to ask if you were doing the interviewing.

Key Terms

appraisal interview. A type of **interview** in which the interviewee's performance is assessed by management or by more experienced colleagues.

BFOQ. Bona fide occupational qualification question, as opposed to questions that are illegal.

cheat sheet. A summary of the items you want to discuss in an interview.

chronological résumé. A type of **résumé** that organizes experience and job titles beginning with the most recent or current position and working back through the work history.

confidence. A quality of interpersonal effectiveness; a comfortable, at-ease feeling in interpersonal communication situations.

cover letter. A letter of introduction that accompanies the résumé.

cultural rule. Rules that are specific to a given cultural group and that members are expected to follow.

cultural sensitivity. An attitude and way of behaving in which you're aware of and acknowledge cultural differences.

curriculum vitae. A type of **résumé** used by professors and scientists that lists their accomplishments, writings, discoveries, and service.

employment interview. A type of **interview** in which the interviewee is questioned to ascertain his or her suitability for a particular job.

exit interview. A type of **interview** in which employees and management discuss the reasons for the employee's leaving the corporation.

expressiveness. A quality of interpersonal effectiveness that consists of genuine involvement in speaking and listening, conveyed verbally and nonverbally.

flexibility. The ability to adjust communication strategies and skills on the basis of the unique situation.

follow-up letters. Letters sent after the interview to thank the interviewer and, in the case of employment interviews, to advance the likelihood of your getting the job (or a job).

functional résumé. A type of **résumé** that organizes experience in terms of competences or skills.

guided interview. An interview structure in which questions are chosen in advance but are treated flexibly, in response to the ongoing interaction.

immediacy. A quality of interpersonal effectiveness that conveys a sense of contact and togetherness, a feeling of interest in and liking for the other person.

informal interview. An interview format that has little formal structure.

information interview. A type of **interview** in which the interviewer asks the interviewee, usually a person of some reputation and accomplishment, questions designed to elicit his or her views, predictions, and perspectives on specific topics.

interaction management. A quality of interpersonal effectiveness in which the interaction is controlled and managed to the satisfaction of both parties; effectively managing conversational turns, fluency, and message consistency.

interview. A particular form of interpersonal communication in which two or more persons interact largely by question-and-answer format to achieve specific goals.

job shadowing. An increasingly common practice of following a person at work to learn what the job entails.

leading question. See **neutral and leading questions.**

leave-taking cues. Verbal and nonverbal cues that indicate a desire to terminate a conversation.

networking. Enlisting the aid of others to help solve a problem, often the problem of finding a job.

neutral and leading questions. A classification of questions based on whether they provide no indication of what the interviewer expects (neutral) or do indicate what the interviewer expects or wants (leading).

open-ended and closed questions. A classification of questions based on the freedom of response allowed, ranging from total freedom (open-ended) to a simple "yes" or "no" (closed).

openness. A quality of interpersonal effectiveness involving a person's willingness to take an active role in the interview whether in asking or answering questions.

other-orientation. A quality of interpersonal effectiveness involving attentiveness, interest, and concern for the other person.

persuasive interview. A type of **interview** in which the interviewer attempts to change the interviewee's attitudes or behavior.

positiveness. A characteristic of interpersonal effectiveness involving positive attitudes and the use of positive messages expressing these attitudes (as in complimenting others), along with acceptance and approval.

primary and follow-up questions. A classification of questions based on whether they introduce a topic (primary) or ask for some additional information on a topic already raised (follow-up).

quantitative interview. A type of interview structure in which response choices are identified in advance so that they can be measured and statistical analysis applied.

résumé. A summary of essential information about your experience, education, and abilities; also see **chronological résumé, functional résumé,** and **curriculum vitae.**

standard open interview. An interview structure designed for interviewing a variety of job candidates and having prearranged and ordered questions that are asked of each applicant.

top-grading interview. An especially intense and detailed interview designed to identify potential top performers.

unlawful questions. Questions that are legally prohibited in a job interview, focusing on, for example, age, arrest record, or religion.

Bibliography

Acor, A. A. (2001). Employers' perceptions of persons with body art and an experimental test regarding eyebrow piercing. PhD dissertation, Marquette University. *Dissertation Abstracts International: Second B: The Sciences and Engineering*, 61, 3885.

Anderson, R., & Killenberg, G. M. (2008). *Interviewing: Speaking, Listening, and Learning for Professional Life*, 2nd ed. New York: Oxford University Press.

Axtell, R. E. (1990). *Do's and taboos of hosting international visitors*. Hoboken, NJ: Wiley.

Axtell, R. E. (1993). *Do's and taboos around the world*, 3rd ed. Hoboken, NJ: Wiley.

Axtell, R. E. (2007). *Essential do's and taboos: The complete guide to international business and leisure travel*. Hoboken, NJ: Wiley.

Barna, L. M. (1991). Stumbling blocks in intercultural communication. In L. A. Samovar & R. E. Porter (Eds.), *Intercultural communication: A reader*, 4th ed. (pp. 345–352). Belmont, CA: Wadsworth.

Copeland, L., & Griggs, L. (1985). *Going international: How to make friends and deal effectively in the global marketplace*. New York: Random House.

DeGroot, T., & Motowidlo, S. J. (1999). Why visual and vocal interview cues can affect interviewers' judgments and predict job performance. *Journal of Applied Psychology*, 84 (December), 986–993.

Dresser, N. (1999). *Multicultural celebrations: Today's rules of etiquette for life's special occasions*. New York: Three Rivers Press.

Dresser, N. (2005). *Multicultural manners: Essential rules of etiquette for the 21st century*, Rev. ed. Hoboken, NJ: Wiley.

Drews, D. R., Allison, C. K., & Probst, J. R. (2000). Behavioral and self-concept differences in tattooed and nontattooed college students. *Psychological Reports*, 86, 475–481.

Forbes, G. B. (2001). College students with tattoos and piercings: Motives, family experiences, personality factors, and perception by others. *Psychological Reports*, 89, 774–786.

Haft, T. (1997). *Résumés*. Princeton, NJ: Princeton Review.

Hambrick, R. S. (1991). *The management skills builder: Self-directed learning strategies for career development*. New York: Praeger.

Kanter, A. B. (1995). *The essential book of interviewing: Everything you need to know from both sides of the table*. New York: Random House [Times Books].

Kennedy, J. L. (2000). *Job interviews for dummies*. New York: Hungry Minds.

Kirby, D. (2001, January 30). Finessing interviews: Don't ask, do tell. *New York Times*, G2.

Powell, L., & Amsbary, J. H. (2006). *Interviewing: Situations and Contexts*. Boston: Allyn & Bacon.

Pullum, S. J. (1991). Illegal questions in the selection interview: Going beyond contemporary business and professional communication textbooks. *Bulletin of the Association for Business Communication*, 54 (September), 36–43.

Rector, M., & Neiva, E. (1996). Communication and personal relationships in Brazil. In W. B. Gudykunst, S. Ting-Toomey, & T. Nishida (Eds.), *Communication in personal relationships across cultures* (pp. 156–173). Thousand Oaks, CA: Sage.

Ruben, B. D. (1985). Human communication and cross-cultural effectiveness. In L. A. Samovar, & R. E. Porter (Eds.), *Intercultural communication: A reader*, 4th ed. (pp. 338–346). Belmont, CA: Wadsworth.

Seidman, I. E. (1991). *Interviewing as qualitative research: A guide for researchers in education and the social sciences*. New York: Teachers College Press.

Snyder, M. (1987). *Public appearances, private realities*. New York: W. H. Freeman.

Spitzberg, B. H. (1991). Intercultural communication competence. In L. A. Samovar & R. E. Porter (Eds.), *Intercultural communication: A reader*, 6th ed. (pp. 353–365). Belmont, CA: Wadsworth.

Spitzberg, B. H., & Cupach, W. R. (2002). Interpersonal skills. In M. L. Knapp & J. A. Daly (Eds.), *Handbook of interpersonal communication*, 3rd ed. (pp. 564–611). Thousand Oaks, CA: Sage.

Stewart, C. J., & Cash, W. B. (2008). *Interviewing: principles and practices*, 12th ed. New York: McGraw-Hill.

Taub, M. (1997). *Interviews*. Princeton, NJ: Princeton Review.

Taylor, J. with Hardy, D. (2005). *Monster careers: Interviewing*. New York: Penguin.

Zincoff, M. Z., & Goyer, R. S. (1984). *Interviewing*. New York: Macmillan.

Index

Note: Page numbers followed by *f*, *t*, and *g* indicate figures, tables, and glossary terms, respectively.